"People in the gay communi ___ ___ to death on so many occasions since the onslaught of the AIDS epidemic that they have become the natural experts on NDEs in our time. They have not only had NDEs themselves but also are surrounded by other people who have had NDEs. These communities are becoming a prototype of what communities might be. We are acutely aware of our own mortality and live from the values learned in an NDE. Dr. Liz Dale's compilation of NDE stories from the gay community is a welcome and timely addition to the NDE literature. Her research into NDEs in the gay community is ground breaking."

Pamela M. Kircher, M.D.
Author of *Love Is The Link*

"*Crossing Over & Coming Home* is a wonderful affirmation of the power and meaning near-death states can have on the experiencer. For the individual, though, it is especially important that a comfortable climate exists for the sharing of their stories. Since no one has done that for the gay community, Liz Dale is to be commended for her sensitivity in this regard."

P. M. H. Atwater, Lh.D.
Near-death researcher since 1978
Author of many books on the subject, especially
Children of the New Millenium
Three Rivers Press, New York City, 1999

"*Crossing Over & Coming Home* is an important book. A pioneering study of near-death experiences in the gay community, it is also a major contribution to the general understanding of the phenomenology of near-death states and their effects on survivors."

Stanislav Grof, M.D.
Author of *The Human Encounter with Death*
and *Beyond the Brain*

Crossing Over
&
Coming Home

Twenty-one Authors
Discuss the Gay Near-Death Experience
as Spiritual Transformation

Liz Dale, Ph.D.

Foreword by Melvin Morse, M.D.

Copyright ©2001 by Liz Dale, Ph.D., R.N., C.H.T.

Published by
    Emerald Ink Publishing, Inc.
        (800) 324-5663
    http://www.emeraldink.com
    E-mail emerald@emeraldink.com

Library of Congress Cataloging-in-Publication Data

    Crossing Over & Coming Home : twenty-one authors discuss the gay
    near-death experience as spiritual transformation / [compiled by] Elizabeth
    Dale; foreword by Melvin Morse.
        p. cm.
    Includes bibliographical references.
    ISBN 1-885373-32-5
    1. Near-Death experiences. 2. Gays--Psychology. 3.
    Lesbians--Psychology. 4. Spiritual life. I. Title: Crossing over and
    coming home. II. Dale, Elizabeth, 1948-
        BF1045.N4 C76 2001
        133.9'01'308664--dc21
                        00-011908

Back & front cover photography and shamanic drawing (page 21)
by Rhonda Olmsted

Printed in USA

Dedication

I thank all the volunteers who donated their NDE stories, sharing their intimate details of other worldliness and trusting the process involved in revealing this material to the world. Thanks to these who came to Delancey Street Restaurant in San Francisco to share their stories in person and help plan various aspects of the book. A great big thanks to Chris Carson of Emerald Ink Publishing who taught us the process of preparing a manuscript, to Linda Hiltabidle for her fine typing and to those who were kind enough to help with reading, editing, endorsing, and preparing the final edition. P. M. H. Atwater, Lh.D., Pamela Kircher, M.D., Stan Grof, M.D., Ken Ring, Ph.D., and Paul Bernstein, Ph.D., contributed in various ways. With special thanks to Melvin Morse, M.D., who prepared the foreword. And where would we be without the general reader? Thanks to all of you for your interest and support in this ground-breaking development and research. Please send all communications to the publisher:

Emerald Ink Publishing
9700 Almeda Genoa #502
Houston, Texas 77075 USA

E-mail: emerald@emeraldink.com
Phone 800-324-5663

To contact the author by e-mail: LizDale1@juno.com
by phone 510.526.7530

Acknowledgments

"I like to walk alone on country paths, rice plants, and wild grasses on both sides, putting each foot down on the earth in mindfulness, knowing that I walk on the wondrous earth."

Thich Nhat Hanh
The Miracle of Mindfulness

"Death is the most important question of our time, as Yale's psychiatrist Robert Jay Lifton has suggested, in good part because we refuse to face it."

Professor Houston Smith
Foreword in *Death And Dying*

"The soul continues to develop in the after-death state. After death some souls go straight to the Divine, while most have attachment to the body and consequently are born into a physical body again. Because one cannot fulfill one's desires in the subtle world, as long as one has desires one must take a body again."

Mother Meera
Mother Meera Answers

To Mother Meera, my spiritual teacher and continual inspiration.

To my partner, Rhonda, for her 25 years of unending love and support.

To Steve Rogers, who served as the Gay NDE volunteer and supported the project since day one.

Contents

FOREWORD

Crossing Over and Coming Home contains the moving and often inspiring near-death experiences of gays and lesbians. So much of what we know about near-death experiences comes from descriptions of the dying experiences of heterosexual Americans of European descent. The near-death experiences that gays and lesbians report are powerful reminders that all human beings share a common truth: We will have near-death experiences when we die. The scientific research on NDEs clearly documents that they are in fact the dying experience. Gay or straight, brown skin or white skin, or rich and poor alike, we will all have one when we die. Those who have had the dying experience and then lived often report that our lives are made meaningful by the loving relationships we form while we are alive. Few report that they learned from their NDE that they didn't make enough money while they were alive or spent enough time pursuing a demanding career.

One important purpose of life is to develop loving relationships. When we die, an important part of the dying process is to reflect on the loving relationships that we had during our life. Those who have had near-death experiences often describe the sudden spiritual realization that love is a prime force in our universe. They report that the power of love is not a meaningless cliché. It is inspiring to realize that at the end of life we learn that love is as fundamental a universal force as the subatomic forces that hold together the building blocks of matter. I find it ironic that these experiences shared in this book taught me so much about what true love is; I felt that I had a better understanding of the love that my wife and I share after reading this book. The loving relationships that gays and lesbians forge during life are often discussed, trivialized, ridiculed, and even angrily denounced by society. This book documents that all loving relationships are nurtured by God's love. Once again, we learn that our most sacred truths are often expressed by the disempowered and disenfranchized among us.

Crossing Over And Coming Home, by presenting gay and lesbian near-death experiences, documents the overarching human experience within the NDE. The death experiences described in this book have the same common themes of NDEs described by middle class Euro-Americans, Native Americans, Japanese children, and even Fundamentalist Christians. We learn from reading this book the importance of intimacy of love for human growth and potential, regardless of lifestyle.

I feel extremely honored to be asked to introduce this book. I marvel at the courage of those who share their experiences with us. These are deeply personal stories that expose the deepest vulnerabilities of the tellers. This book has enormous value in archiving gay and lesbian near-death experiences, yet after reading just 30 pages, I realized it is not about gay and lesbian NDEs at all. It is a book about people who have chosen to love each other, have earned love and respect from like-minded souls, and who deserve love. I have a better understanding of how I can be a more loving person after reading this book.

I have a more personal reason for my gratitude in being asked to introduce this book. I have been struggling with grief over the many friends I have had who have died of AIDS, and the children I have cared for who have AIDS. I cared for many hemophiliacs when I was in training as a physician: almost all of them have died of AIDS. Those fragile children usually had the brightest smiles and the greatest joy in living. They often provided me with the inspiration to make it through one more day of grueling residency training.

I was enormously comforted to read the stories of those who had AIDS or who shared the dying experiences of those with AIDS. Those who die young frequently know secrets of life that cannot be learned in any other way. This book is also about the healing power of spiritual experiences. The tragedy of the AIDS epidemic contains within it these inspiring stories of love and spiritual understanding. I thank Dr. Dale for the courage and vision to share these experiences with us.

Melvin Morse, M.D.

INTRODUCTION

In August of 1996, I attended the annual conference of the International Association for Near-Death Studies (IANDS) in Oakland, California. A plenary speaker was discussing a small research project she had completed on AIDS and cancer patients who had near-death experiences (NDEs). She mentioned that no research existed on the NDE within the gay community and encouraged researchers in the IANDS community to think about doing some research in this area. I left the conference motivated to work on a study in San Francisco, my current residence.

I had completed a number of research studies during my years of schooling prior to obtaining my Ph.D. in clinical psychology at a private school in San Francisco. The most challenging project was an HIV-related chart review of psychiatric patients who had been seen in a local psychiatric emergency room. The project began in 1983 and led to the dissertation entitled *"A Chart Review of HIV High Risk Patients Seen In A Psychiatric Emergency Service.*"

When I arrived home from the IANDS conference, I looked for literature dealing with the gay NDE and, as the speaker had inferred, I found that no studies existed. I proceeded to write a questionnaire which summarizes common themes that one experiences in an NDE. I also wrote a consent form which covered confidentiality and anonymity. At that point, I contacted the gay community through a popular local newspaper. One of the editors ran a story asking for participants who would rise to the challenge of being among the first individuals to participate in such a study. I also ran an ad in IANDS monthly magazine, *Vital Signs*, looking for participants among the IANDS membership. Over a two year period, more than 30 people came forward with their stories.

In the fall of 1997, our small group began to meet on a monthly basis at a local restaurant. The focus was not only to discuss the project, but also to begin face to face storytelling about each of our NDEs. Each month we discussed ways the NDE has affected our lives, honored all newcomers and encouraged them to come forward with anything they felt comfortable sharing. Some group members had never told of their experiences before.

The feeling of having such a group is incredibly liberating. Members felt listened to at a very deep level. During our discussions, all other experiences that parallel the NDE were also shared. For instance, it is not uncommon to hear about some type of psychic event someone has had since their NDE.

Over two years have passed now, and our group has decided to publish these incredible stories of their near-death experiences. One member of the group, Chris Carson, who responded to the ad in the *San Francisco Bay Area Reporter,* is one of the publishers at Emerald Ink in Houston, Texas. We want to thank him for participating in this project and for enthusiastically taking on the publication of our book, *Crossing Over and Coming Home.*

In summary, this book is a collection of our stories about the NDE and related topics. I trust you will find the book to be both heartwarming and exciting. This book belongs in the library of anyone interested in alternative realities, non-ordinary states of consciousness, and those who find the world of the spirit to be mysteriously intriguing.

Heal The World

Amy is a middle school teacher who teaches health and science. She has been out of the closet since age 15, is currently 38 years of age. She collects wild mushrooms for her hobby and enjoys adventure sports, like white water rafting. She is very involved in community activism in regards to human rights and gay/lesbian/straight education networks (GLSEN) in San Mateo, California.

My near-death experience made me feel like I had a purpose here on earth, a destiny, that I had not yet fulfilled. It made me feel important.

I was drinking and someone told a joke which caused me to laugh rather than swallow—as a result, I choked, passed out, and hit my head. Next, I felt like I was dreaming—I saw short film clips of my life flash before me: my eighth birthday up in the tree house, quick instant reliving of these moments and then I started to go up, as if I was floating up towards a light. It felt wonderful, but in the distance I heard my sister say, "Oh my God, she's turning blue!" Then I put on the brakes. I stopped drifting to the light (even though it was still very tempting because it felt so wonderful). Something inside me shouted, "NO! I'm not ready yet." My friend had just seen on TV the day before the Heimlich maneuver and together we worked to come back into my body. I had the will and he had the skill, so to speak. Everyone was worried about me as if something terrible had happened, but I felt great. I had a sense of purpose and I wasn't afraid to die.

During this time, I was in a tunnel and I felt surrounded by souls who loved me. It was as if I were traveling through space like a floating spirit. The light was bluish and looked a little like moonlight, but I resisted the light because I understood it to be the point of no return. I felt that it wasn't time yet; I wasn't done. I had more to do.

I saw other familiar people/entities/animals, but unidentifiable. The people were loving and caring, as if they were relatives who died that I really hadn't known.

When I came back, I felt a peace within me always, a piece of God or the light.

Today, in my dreams I have stopped flying; now I just drift.

In this experience, I have learned I have a purpose, something important I'm supposed to do for society. I learned that death feels wonderful. I know there is another dimension that I can access if I need to. I feel like there is something special about me. At times, I feel like an observer even when I'm participating. I check to see if I am supposed to be where I am. I have more intuitive guidance. Many situations feel wrong now—crowds, downtown—and I avoid them. I listen to the voice within. I trust it. Today, I am a teacher and it feels like I'm where I'm supposed to be. I fight injustices daily and teach kids to respect each other. I feel like I'm doing my part to "heal the world."

In summary, my NDE was at age 15. I was on the wrong path. I was making some poor choices at that time and wasn't sure whether I'd live to see my thirties. I was pretty reckless. It did a few things to me, or for me. I realized that I lived for a reason, that I had some greater goal to accomplish that I had not accomplished yet.

It also gave me a great sense of peace around dying. I wasn't afraid to die anymore. I think I'm on the right track now and the idea of dying is not scary for me. I think it will be a beautiful experience when my time is right.

1. Did sexual identity come into play during your NDE?

No.

2. After the NDE, did the near-death experience change your sexual identify in any way or change the way you feel about your sexual identity?

No.

A VOID OF LIGHTNESS

Dorothy is a secretary on the board of the women's AIDS network and the editor of the newsletter in San Francisco. She is also a counsel member on the Mayor's Planning Council for people with AIDS.

My near-death experience happened in New York in 1988. I was on the table in the emergency room at Bronx Lebanon Hospital. I did not know I was there. I felt like I was floating in a void of lightness and it felt peaceful, then I became agitated and said, "No, No, No." I felt like I was outside my body looking down as I heard the doctors say, "We lost her; there's no heart beat." I could see them putting stimulators on me to jerk a heart beat out of me. I did not feel any of the pounding or massaging they did on my chest, but I thought they heard my cries. I was mistaken and realized I was talking to someone else, saying, "I'm not ready yet. I have too much work to do!" Then I heard them asking about next of kin and for ID. I continued to be panicky and fearful saying, "No, No, No," The next thing I knew, I felt a vacuum pulling me down into darkness, then up into my lungs and I began to breath harder and harder. I knew I needed to get off this table and get back my life, so I pulled the

IV out of my neck and I left. I said, "I have too much work to do yet in this lifetime!"

In summary, I knew there was more work that I had to do, that my life was pre-planned. I would come to the West Coast and devote my life to helping people with AIDS and other life-threatening diseases. It would be a great learning experience and I could be a great teacher. That is the way it has turned out.

1. Did sexual identity come into play during your NDE?

No.

2. After the NDE, did the near-death experience change your sexual identify in any way or change the way you feel about your sexual identity?

No.

LEAVING THIS WORLD & RETURNING SAFELY

My NDE experience happened when I was three-years old. I ate or sniffed bleach. Then my father was very upset. Mother and my aunt were in the kitchen. We lived in Berkeley during that time. Mother claimed we had just come back from a two-week vacation in San Antonio, Texas. My older brother Larry also began getting sick. I became deathly sick and heavy with fluids on my lungs. My parents took me to Doctor's Hospital in Pinole, California. The doctors asked if I drank or ate something. Mother was not sure. Then I was sent to Children's Hospital in Oakland, California where I was pronounced dead from heart failure and edema to the lungs for 15 minutes. I remember my aunt praying over me telling them I was not dead. After 15 minutes, I awoke out of this sleep. I could hear my aunt screaming, "Thank you, Jesus, he's not dead!" This miracle was in the *Oakland Gazette*, and I survived.

Then, in 1995, my lover died. The day he died, I had a rushing feeling. I was hysterical. I knew something was deadly wrong. The very next day, I found out he was dead.

In 1982, I was 18 years old. I had been seeking help with alcohol and speed abuse. My friend gave me some drugs one particular day and I felt good the first few hours of the day. That night, I began feeling numb and a feeling of dying slowly came over me. I remember hearing bells and a slight vision of light coming toward me. I do remember hearing strange noises and I felt a certain spirit coming over me. I began to scream and fight for consciousness. I gripped my hands tightly together and gradually I came out of near-death. Since then, I have been attending AA meetings. I feel that my life is going to be more positive. I have been living alone and taking better care of myself. I was very cautious of all people, evil and good, and I pray to God everyday to become stronger and more accepting.

In June, 1994, I was living in San Francisco. I was fully gay and out. I had a very few friends who were gay and they had HIV or AIDS. I still associated myself with them even though, at the time, I was HIV negative. One weekend they invited me to have alcoholic drinks. They shot speed and had a party. I told them I didn't want to go home that particular night because we were in the Tenderloin late at night. They let me sleep on the floor beside their bed. I was drunk and felt somewhat sick, feeling like I was losing life. I heard them talking and felt a sort of losing life. After ten seconds, I regained my life. Again, I saw light speeding fast around my body. It was a kind of wicked spirit around these people and I got up and left and went home. I'll never forget leaving this world and returning safely.

Dying Can Be Peaceful

Dr. Ruth is a family physician who specializes in Palliative Care. She is currently working at Victoria Hospice in Victoria, British Columbia.

I had been having neurological problems and had been diagnosed as having *myasthenia gravis* (turned out I didn't). But at the time I was the most ill, I had lost use of many muscle groups and was rushed to a hospital emergency room. I was feeling very weird and was having trouble talking. I don't really know what happened next, except that all of a sudden I was floating horizontally up by the ceiling. I looked down and could see my mother sitting by the side of the bed, towards my feet, and a young blond doctor in a white coat who was getting a trach tube ready. As I looked down, it was as though I was looking through a scrim or a net. I could see what was happening, but it was veiled. I was very comfortable, and it was very light. I saw light all around and just floated in space, high up by the ceiling. I thought to myself, "Oh, I must be dying. This isn't so bad." I remember being amazed that I was not frightened; I had always thought I would be frightened to die. I felt amazingly calm as I watched my mother. I felt such pain for her. As I watched the blond doctor busying himself with the tray I was very comfortable. All of a sudden I thought, "Hey, if I'm dying, then I will never see Maria (my then partner) again." That was it. The next thing I remember was the next day, when I woke up in ICU.

In reality, I was apparently unconscious when I was in the emergency room. I later found out from my mom that there was indeed a young blond doctor who was just about to perform a tracheotomy when I guess I began to breathe on my own.

Now I realize dying can be peaceful and not terrifying.

SHOW THEM THE WAY

In November, 1975, I drove into a wall. I remember as my jaw hit the steering wheel I said, "Oh, shit! I'm dead!" and then I was. Apparently, I was taken to a major trauma hospital. I was not conscious but I vividly remember looking up and seeing some number above a door, although my glasses had been lost and I am very near-sighted. Twenty years ago, I could have told you the number, but now it is lost to me. I looked down on my body and remember being in a dark tunnel moving along somehow. I was not in pain or discomfort. I do not remember any details in the darkness, but the light was visible and growing.

Then I was surrounded by light so intense I could feel it. I could not look—it just sort of permeated me. I felt this enormous love and well-being—peace, if you will. I had some sense of omniscience, or knowing everything. I felt that everything was right—as it should be. There was a purpose to everything. I felt knowledge and glimpsed godhood, I guess. There was absolute understanding, absolute love, absolute peace. Next I turned away and communication began with what others call a gatekeeper or angel or Jesus, but it was someone. If I ever knew, I cannot remember now.

I heard that God depended on us to work on earth. Intervention was not an option, somehow. I remember an explanation of Hell and Purgatory, though I am not Catholic nor was I previously concerned with Purgatory. Once I wrote a story in eighth grade about the guard at the crossing of the River Styxx. I heard that actually there is no purgatory and no hell. People who leave too soon or hurt others may (must?) watch what effect their actions have on others. Time is so different there. Watching the results can be painful, I understood, but I did not understand it to be mandatory. I just understood it—no heaven or hell. The good ones get to watch, too.

I learned that plans existed for me and that I had altered those plans by suicide. I could (or must?) go back. There was much to do. I remember not exactly wanting to leave, but not resisting, either. Having seen the other side, I complied agreeably somehow and was imparted with these last words: "Show them the way."

I remember somehow telling my heart to start beating: we had work to do, and I woke up in a bright light with medical people cutting on me and wiring my jaws. I remember their asking if it hurt and I said, "Yes." They told me they hadn't used a pain-killer as I had been in shock.

They asked me if I wanted relief now. I felt the pain, but in a new and different way. I said, "No" and I was *glad* to have the pain somehow, but it was only a ghost of other pain I had felt. Later they moved me to a bed and strapped me into traction. I had fractured my jaw, suffered a concussion, fractured ribs and dislocated my hip. My face looked like a Frankenstein, split between the lip and chin all the way to both ears, cuts and wounds all over. But I was at peace. They gave Demerol for pain. My hip really hurt. A Methodist minister came to me in the room and spoke down to me. I was offended. I had just had the most powerful experience of my life and he was telling me some bull. I told him I was an atheist—leave me alone, and he did.

I went home to my parents during recovery. I drank bloody marys and malted milks through my wired jaws. When I got better and returned to work, I returned to my old ways. I quit the job and took a bicentennial tour of America. I remember at the Washington National Cemetery, as I walked by a huge oak tree in the Confederate section, I heard wailing and screaming and sadness of great depth, though there was no one around me. I remember crying in the hot noontime sun while walking to JFK's eternal flame. There, too, I was moved emotionally in rare depth. I felt the presence of many souls.

In 1983, I sold in-home products nightly. I lived with a relative I loved dearly and we both drank. I remember worrying as she suffered more and more. One Thursday night in July of 1983, I ran to my appointment at a home isolated in the woods. They bought my goods but insisted I eat with them. They questioned me and found my troubled concerns. They said they would pray for my relative. Friday night I caroused. Saturday, I worked all day. I remember coming home to a smoke-filled house. My relative was carrying chicken frying in the skillet while an old school friend of hers ran from the house screaming that she couldn't take the craziness anymore. I could not communicate with my relative and left. I stayed at the Chief Motel on Main Street where I bought a big bottle of red wine and lots of cigarettes and watched television all night by myself. I went home Sunday night. My relative was asleep. I slept rock-solid and left early the next day to work. That afternoon, four days or so after the strangers prayed, my relative admitted herself to the hospital. I was overjoyed that night that she was getting help, so glad I fixed myself a bloody mary and then another and another.

One month later, I slept through a small hurricane in Houston. It came through that night and I was sleeping drunk—missed the whole thing. In Family Week the next week, therapists convinced me that I needed to go to a recovery program, too, so I did. I attended my first meeting at a gay chapter where I have been going ever since. That was 1983.

Since that time, I have had a feeling that someone was with me, always. I have only once or twice felt briefly left alone. I started a business, my own, and struggled. I remember a year after a powerful relationship with a lover broke up that I was lonely. I remember praying to God for something specific. One of the steps states that we pray to our higher power only for knowledge of his will for us and the power to carry that out. That night, I prayed for someone to love, someone who could love me, too. The next week, I met a man with eyes that shone. I knew he was the one. We have been together ever since. I cannot tell you how much he has meant to me, to my recovery, to my success, to my future. He has understood me at my worst and stood beside me in acceptance. He does not know for himself the spiritual feelings that I have, but he accepts them as true for me. He is my gift from God and I have done as well by him as I am able.

My old drinking friends are all dead except one and she has one more year of sobriety than I do. What is it like now for me? My physical scars are almost all gone. I have my own business. I am a member of the community, active in civic affairs through a service organization. I own a house and beachhouse, trade the commodity markets, travel and read, love and live. I ache in strange spots as I age. I am always aware that my pains are *my* doing. My father died loving me and I loved him. We were friends, if not always in agreement. My Mother died a year later in my arms, peacefully, surrounded by her grown children and little grandchildren. My friends died loving me and I them. I have made new friends and my lover grows more important to me daily. I know now what I glimpsed so many years ago and I have it here with me. May you have it, too.

1. Did sexual identity come into play during your NDE?

Not really. I felt loved by the light and I felt fine, guiltless when I awoke. I understood that God had made me and therefore I was perfect as a raw material. I could reach people no one else could, with my unique experiences and outlook. I came back OK with myself, though no specific questions or answers passed between us on this subject.

2. After the NDE, did the near-death experience change your sexual identity in any way or change the way you feel about your sexual identity?

Yes. Once, the "Straight Slate" in Houston was trying to get people elected on homophobia. One of the families down the street from my parents had asked my father to contribute, but he turned them down firmly. I went down there and introduced myself, adding that I understood they were raising funds for the Straight Slate. Then I asked, "Have you ever met a homosexual?" They said no, and I replied, "Well, you have now!" They lost in the elections and both died a year later.

In business, when I meet a potential client and we get down to the part where they sign, I add one more thing. I tell them I'm gay and if that is a problem working with me in the future, I understand and they can and should walk away now. I have never had anyone stop there, but I have a great many begin to know me honestly. It has been great.

You Are Dead! It's OK!

Liz is a clinical psychotherapist/hypnotherapist/nurse who works in private practice in Albany, California and at San Francisco General Hospital in the psychiatric emergency room. Since her NDE, she has been interested in hypnosis, shamanism, holotropic breath work, and studying Buddhism as well as other world religions.

As a child, I had a number of unusual experiences that made very little sense to me at the time. I was interested in religion, had been raised Catholic and loved the rituals of the Latin masses. I was drawn towards the ornamentation of various churches and could meditate for long periods while using such stimuli as the sun flowing through stained glass windows in various cathedrals. I spoke to Jesus often, left food out on a picnic table (just in case He was hungry) and checked on a regular basis to see if He came by to eat. This was in grade school. In high school, I found myself being able to move into trance states by simply lying quietly and going deeply inside. I found the experience frightening and yet exciting, although I had no idea what it meant to be pulled into some other realm.

By the time I was in college, I had spent many years reading psychology, theology, and philosophy. I had never heard of the near-death experience at the time I went over to the other side. The year was 1967. I was a freshman at the University of Wisconsin at LaCrosse, living directly across the street from the university in campus housing. I drove my motorcycle across the Mississippi River one summer afternoon, my boyfriend riding on the back. We were coming home from Winona, Minnesota. I felt a stinging feeling on my upper right thigh area, but initially thought little of it. Wisconsin is full of stinging insects, so a welt forming on my leg was nothing unusual. By the time I parked the bike, I realized I felt unusually itchy. I went to my room, one house away from my boyfriend and began to feel more and more uncomfortable. Hives began to develop on my arms and legs. Itching was intense. I tore off my clothing, went to fill the tub, hoping to get relief from being in a tub of water.

Although my boyfriend had never been to my rented room, suddenly he arrived and lifted me out of the tub. He threw a towel over me and carried me to the university emergency room directly behind campus housing. I was incredibly frightened, fighting for my life. I began to realize that my breathing was also being affected. I had no idea what anyone was doing as far as my treatment. Nor did I hear anyone talking to me. I did feel this incredible fear that I was about to die. I began to realize that, despite the most intense attempts at breathing, I was not getting any air into my lungs. I was in a state of total panic.

Some kind of relief flooded over me when I heard a voice say, "You are dead! It's OK!" Instantly, I was transported to a new place, leaving my body behind on the ER table. I flew effortlessly through the ceiling and found myself standing in a magnificent field of tall grass. The grass was glistening, flowing in a slight breeze. The colors of the sky and grass were such that I had never seen before. I saw myself in a flowing dress of some kind and was dancing with my mother who wore the same kind of attire. She was an adult, I was a small child, maybe nine or ten years old. I felt an incredible relief. My mother had died four years before this time and I was very glad to see her. We did not talk, only danced. We were incredibly happy. Just as suddenly, I was sent back into my body on the emergency room table. I heard a doctor who leaned over very close to me and say, "That was very close!" The treatments continued for some time, going through over 45 injections of adrenaline over a couple of hours. Finally, I was released. In the middle of dinner (that same day), I suddenly needed to return to the ER when the hives and shortness of breath returned. Again, I needed additional medication. A few years later, I went to an allergist who informed me that, should I get stung by two bees at once, nothing could resuscitate me. He did attempt to desensitize me with small amounts of antigen. The smallest amount threw me into a state of panic, hives returned once again and the treatment was discontinued.

It took me many years to fully process this event. Initially, I did not share my experience with anyone for fear they would think I was strange. I guess I felt this otherworldly experience was a one-of-a-kind event. I had no idea many others had had a similar experience in their own NDE. I had other types of psychic phenomena after the NDE. For instance, I was camping outside with a friend a few years later when my mother appeared to me. She was standing on the top of a hill and looked displeased about something.

Over the years, I have been more and more impressed at my total lack of fear of death. This feeling also extends itself into a lack of interest in many of this life's realities. For instance, I have been totally unimpressed with people's feelings of self-importance. I have realized that hierarchies are only man-made. They mean essentially nothing. I realize that someone or something (I call God or Goddess) has a special understanding of each of us, and has plans for each of us that we need to carry out to be fully realized. I remember finally, many years after my NDE, discovering the works of Raymond Moody, Kenneth Ring, PMH Atwater and others who have researched NDEs extensively.

Another important event in my life since the NDE was a weekend workshop on shamanism led by Michael Harner in August, 1996. After we asked a health-related question and the drumming began, I experienced a visual representation of being cut longitudinally from head to toe. I was laid out, wide open. Something reached inside of my body and threw out my intestines into the space above my body. The entrails were sucked into some other reality, as if by some giant vacuum cleaner. I then was placed back together and immediately fed through some kind of meat grinder which produced a large bowl of meat (which I knew was me). Amazingly, it was not frightening, I had no actual physical feeling attached to the event. Michael Harner asked if anyone had a healing or a cure during their journey and I did not respond. I was in a kind of psychological shock—not frightened, but incredibly surprised by what I had witnessed. I didn't realize at the time that this was the start of a journey towards wellness. My partner, who had been at the workshop with me, drew a picture of what she perceived was my experience before I told her about it. In the drawing, you can see the focus on the intestinal area.

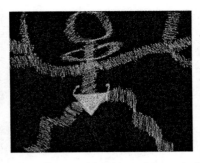
The following events clarified what I had experienced in the shamanic journey. A couple of months after the workshop, I was informed by my OB-GYN physician that I had a type of uterine cancer. It had sprung up rather suddenly and I was scheduled for surgery as soon as the lab results were confirmed. The surgery went well. My surgeon informed me that she might need to refer me to an oncologist for radiation/chemotherapy should the procedure warrant it. Over the next two years, I had regular check ups. Each time, the results come back completely normal. Part of the reason for the total recovery came to me during a holotrophic workshop led by Stan Grof one month after the surgery. I saw a large golden object in the area above the left side of my body. I recognized the object as God and reached up towards it. As my hand reached upward, a golden hand reached down and touched mine. I witnessed the hand actually entering my body, going through a place in the middle of my left hip. No pain was experienced. I saw the hand actually bring something out of my pelvic area, but I was not able to identify what it was. I again felt a flood of relief and a closeness to God that is hard to describe. I told Stan Grof about the event afterwards. He told me he was amazed by the light flowing out of my eyes.

What a journey! I can only say thank you to the Gods and Goddesses who watch over us every day of our lives. I also feel grateful to those humans who are open enough to be able to help us move in the right direction, in our movement back to God.

I am busy working on projects related to this book. For the gay NDE study to be scientific, we need a larger group of people. I'm looking into getting the project onto the internet. I want to thank all of you for your interest in this project. If you have a gay NDE experience, go to www.NDERF.org and share your story. Thank you for your interest in this area of exploration.

1. Did sexual identity come into play during your NDE?

None.

2. After the NDE, did the near-death experience change your sexual identify in any way or change the way you feel about your sexual identity?

After my NDE, I began to reconsider a number of issues including various relationships I was involved in. I had been dating a couple of different men prior to the NDE. Very shortly after the NDE, I broke off contact with these people and remained free of any relationships for about one year. After that, I began to move towards a long standing relationship with a woman I met when I was in nurses' training. This relationship lasted five and one-half years. Prior to my NDE, I had had some sexual feelings towards women, but had not had any actual physical contact with women till after I broke off my relationships with the men I had been dating. I am currently with a woman I met in Cheyenne, Wyoming. We have been together now for over 25 years and are deeply in love.

THE BRIGHTEST STARS

Although my NDE was a peak experience, the circumstances that caused the NDE (Guillian-Barre Syndrome) were most unpleasant. During my NDE, I did not pass through a "tunnel"—I experienced seeing in all directions at once—the blackest sky with billions of the brightest stars in all directions. I was more "conscious" than I had ever felt before, but had no body. The stars increased in intensity until all was light. The people I saw during the experience had previously been deceased. They each welcomed me with a message of love and welcome, peace and happiness, but with no words, as I passed them each toward the increasing light. The light was billions of the brightest stars seen in all directions at once and increasing in intensity until all was light. "White" is inadequate to describe the color, but the closest English word.

I have not noticed a change in my dream life. My dream life has always been a very significant and meaningful part of my life. I always have had occasional precognitive dreams. The NDE was a much more "conscious" experience than either dreams or waking life.

Since my NDE experience, my attitude, concept, and experience of spirituality have increased, but I have no interest in pursuing spirituality. I am cautious and careful about sharing my NDE experience. I share only with people who might appreciate it and only in the right time and circumstances. I try not to waste energy by "casting pearls before the swine."

BEAUTIFUL
SHINING EYES

Andre, a sound and light technician and rock and roll musician, resides in San Francisco with his lover of four years, Russell.

On the days prior to my death in 1991, I can remember feeling a distinct sense of foreboding and familiarity. It seemed like a lot of the gloom and doom prophecy that I chose to believe at the time was playing itself out. I can remember feeling like something big was happening and that I somehow stumbled upon it, only too late. My usual easy going nature had given way to pessimism and extreme self doubt. I can remember waking up that Tuesday morning feeling old, really old and tired. I felt that despite all my best intentions and abilities, I had gotten nowhere. And I believed this to be due to my lack of self discernment. All I knew at the time was that I wanted real change in my life. I felt it was too late.

Sunday, February 14 started off with a bang. My lover, Robert, and I had a terrible argument, over what I can't remember, but I'm sure it had something to do with drugs. At the time we were trying to stop indulging and this led to many arguments and fights. Our relationship had been through a lot in the 10 years we had been together. It was unusually strained at this time. Although we loved and cared for each other, it wasn't enough.

The drugs made it hard to communicate. Well, for some reason, we had a heated argument that resulted in Robert's decision to stay with some good friends in Guerneville for a couple of days. Our good friends, Julie and Renee, were always there to help and they came right away to pick Robert up. I can still remember their driving away that morning with Robert in the back seat and thinking things were never going to be the same. There was a nagging sense of doom. I felt a slight throbbing pain in my gut.

Monday, February 15 ended with a bang. *Huh Lucy Nation*, the band that I had worked so hard at for the past two years unexpectedly split up after a concert in Oakland. This also was due to drugs and miscommunication. The lead guitarist was too doped up to perform and this created quite a spectacle. This incident led to the other members of my band resigning, much to my dismay. I remember feeling really depressed on the ride back home after the show.

Although I had sworn off using drugs just two days before, I found myself at the front door of the neighborhood drug dealer. I must have looked really bad because he told me this would be the last bag of speed he would sell me. I guess this really got to me because on my way home I threw the whole bag away even though I had spent my last $20 on it. I went home even more depressed and went to bed. The pain in my gut seemed to get a bit more uncomfortable.

Tuesday, February 16. I awoke that morning feeling really old. I came to the realization that I needed a radical change in my life—and I needed it *now*. I could no longer go on the way I had been and had no idea where to go next. In a few short months I would be 30 years old and I felt like I had gotten nowhere in my life. I was really depressed and extremely down on myself. I saw all the changes I needed to make but felt I lacked the time to make them. I remember looking in the mirror and saying to myself that I was not in control any more and this scared me. The pain in my lower right gut began to get more painful. Not knowing what it was I figured it was due to my lack of appetite. I tried to eat something later that afternoon, but found it to taste metallic; it had a chemical taste. I also felt extremely fatigued and decided to take a little nap.

Tuesday evening, February 16, I awoke to the sounds of a car horn blowing. I was a little disoriented at first but realized it was 4:00 p.m. and I had slept a little longer than I had anticipated. The car horn blew again and I realized it was Marcus, our other roommate, returning from visiting his parents. Marcus was a good friend and, as usual, he was in an upbeat mood. I was really happy to see him and wanted to talk awhile. But he was just stopping in to pick up his work uniform since he was due at work at 5:00 p.m. I remember feeling extremely dismayed and depressed and not wanting him to know it. So I tried to stay upbeat until he left. I remember feeling a bit panicky as he pulled out of the driveway. The depression seemed to increase as the car moved further away.

Then something weird started happening. It seemed to get darker with every passing moment. Not only dark, but heavy and foreboding. I began going through the entire house and turning on all the lights, but to no avail—it seemed like no matter how many lights I turned on, it remained dull. It was as if the electricity was working at 50%.

I remember wishing I had someone to talk to, *anybody* to talk to; I just did not want to be alone. So I began to look through my phone book for someone to call, but could barely make out people's names. I began to get frantic but tried to calm myself down. I realized I could barely see. It seemed like the same darkness that was occurring outside of me was also inside of me. I began also to notice a hum in my head. My mind became to buzz with chatter. Then, all of a sudden, I felt under attack by waves of self-pity and self-doubt. The chatter got louder and louder, accusing, convicting, shaming, with the volume of the chatter increasing. The pain at my side became unbearable at this time; it, too, was alive with activity.

At this point, I was out of my mind. I began to recite the Lord's Prayer in an effort to calm myself down, but could never seem to finish it with the loud voices that seemed to yell at me over the chatter. The loudest voices seemed to repeat over and over my own self doubts. Once again I set about trying to recite the Lord's Prayer, knowing that its completion could save me. At this time, my head began to quake. I said out loud, "Into your hands, Father." I felt a snapping sound and heard, "I know who you are…get off of him!" Then I felt bliss. It was then that I saw something swirly and hard to describe leave me. All of a sudden, my head stopped buzzing and my lower right gut for the moment stopped throbbing. And I had this overwhelming sense of calm. I felt safe and taken care of. It was as if God had saved me. One thing for sure, something had protected me. The lights still seemed to be operating at 50%, but I seemed to be a lot more optimistic. Since my side felt a little better, at 11:11 pm, I drifted off to sleep watching television.

Wednesday, February 17, I awakened to the television blaring bad news. I remember waking up feeling like I was leaving all this. Marcus had returned from work and was sleeping in his room. I remember smelling a faint odor in the air, a weird chemical smell and wanting to just get away from it. Every channel on the TV seemed to confirm that it was the end of the world and we had better run for the hills. I knew Julie and Renee would be soon dropping Bobby off and that I would then ask them to return us all to Guerneville. Somehow, I just knew inside that they would do this if I asked them. I can remember that my side once again began to pound and that once again I started to lose my sight. I remember waiting for them to get there and, after awhile, they finally did show up.

On Wednesday, February 17, at noon I was sitting in the back seat of Julie and Renee's car with Robert feeling strangely comfortable and complete. And also confused. I remember feeling so calm and conflicted all at the same time, as we pulled out from the driveway. But, one thing for sure, I was glad to be leaving and heading toward Guerneville. It sounded like heaven to me! I can still remember the first raindrops hitting the windshield. As soon as we hit Highway 29, it turned into quite a rainstorm. I remember it was then that I knew something was wrong. The pain in my side returned with such severity that I just fell back in the seat. I sort of watched everything that was going on because no one seemed to be listening when I said I was in pain. They just said, "Sit back and relax." I remember wanting to scream, but I knew they wouldn't listen, so I just held it in. The rain came down so hard on the car that it felt like it was beating in cadence with my side. This, too, freaked me out.

Wednesday, February 17, 1:00 p.m. was when I realized that the faster the rain came down, the faster the pounding in my gut. I was amazed! We seemed to be just speeding down the highway with this tremendous rainstorm beating down on us as we entered forested side roads of north coast heading toward Guerneville. Also, at this time I began to notice the chemical smell was replaced with this flowery (or something sweeter) scent which seemed to be coming from everywhere. It was a deep woodsy, flowery, fruity smell. I remember smelling it and thinking it was the best smell I had ever encountered. It was then I said to myself, "There is something happening here." Just like that, on the radio the first strains of *For What It's Worth* began to play, "There is something happening here." I knew the jig was up. I screamed, "What is going on?" I fell even further back in the seat. I looked at the clock. It was 1:11 p.m.

Then I noticed everyone else in the car knew what was going on, so I attempted to calm myself down. I just watched them and I heard Renee say, "This is where this lady pulled out in front of me and I almost hit her." I thought nothing of it until minutes later she said it again, "This is where this lady pulled out in front of me and I almost hit her." Now this was odd, so I sat up in the seat and looked at the clock and it again said 1:11 p.m. Renee once again repeated her statement. I was totally bewildered but felt energized. We approached the bend and Renee said it yet again, only this time turned around in her seat. Without opening her mouth, she said, "This is where this lady pulled out in front of me and. . ."

The entire car filled up with a scent so heavenly and intoxicating that everything began to blur together. Everything began to glow and shimmer. The pounding of the rain on the car began beating up through the floorboards resulting in this incredible vibration that felt like a full blown orgasm starting at my toes and working its way up my entire body. The pounding! My side began to feel like someone knocking! I once again fell back in my seat.

I heard a voice declaring "I stand at the door and knock." That was when I really began to sink into this entire experience. I then noticed everyone in the car had these beautiful shining eyes and talked without using their mouths. When they did say something, that very same heavenly scent came forth. All of a sudden, I was in rapture.

At this point, I was aware that I no longer needed to use my mouth and began to communicate with these beings with my mind. It was apparent that they were not who I thought they were, so I asked them what had happened. They said that I died Tuesday afternoon when I laid down for a nap. I asked them, "What was the cause?" They said, "A ruptured appendix." Then I remembered the pain in my side and sighed. I remember thinking that it felt great to be dead! Then they asked me if I knew where I was going. I told them I didn't know and then they asked me where did I want to go. I said, "Heaven," and they said, "Good, because that's where we were going." They then asked me, "Where is Heaven?" and I answered, "Heaven is a place on earth," and they shook their heads, "No."

At 2:22 p.m. the roadway looked like a tree-topped tunnel as we drove through what seemed like lifetimes in my mind; we reflected on my entire life. Both my achievements as well as my failures were an open canvas. I knew that in many instances these same beings had intersected my life in many different forms and in numerous ways. I began to feel old as I let out a breath and realized that I, too, gave out this heavenly scent from deep in my soul. I heard the words, "All human beings are good." I remembered feeling glad that I was alive. With every person, we would reminisce about others back on earth. With every face, I could see how we were all connected and that we always were and always would be. One day everyone would be together in heaven, just not now. I remembered how much I loved everyone and they said that not all these people loved you and they let me feel it. The vibration sped up and the car began to accelerate up a steep incline.

At 3:33 p.m., I began to get sad about leaving and began to exhibit a little doubt—not anything I said, but more in the way of feelings. They then took me further back. I can't explain now, but there became this knowing—I had known these beings forever—like a million years or more. It's very hard to explain now, but it was very easy *then* while it was happening. We went into an extensive question and answer session, with each correct answer leading further up the incline. I found that when I just answered from the heart, we began gaining speed. When I hesitated and answered according to what I thought they wanted to hear, we would begin to slow down and go in circles. It took me awhile, but I realized they trusted me enough to simply let me answer from the heart. Now I began to sit up straight in my seat. The air was bursting again and again with this heavenly scent and my entire body began to pulsate and throb.

4:44 p.m. Once again we began to review my life. This time, I could see all the self-doubt that I had in my life centered around the question of my being of any worth to God, since I was a gay man. It was then that I mustered up the courage to ask these beings something I could sense they were waiting for me to ask. I asked, "*Is it okay to be gay?*" and they laughed and said, "Who do you think made gay people?" I remember all of us laughing for what seemed like 1000 years. I felt like I fit in for the first time in my entire life—completely fit in. They then said, "Let's go home." They asked if I knew the secret word and I said I didn't know. They then asked me what it was that I loved to fix for my guests. I said, "Chicken." They said, *"That's the magic word."* So we began to climb to the top of a steep incline. I began to get a little scared because I was always afraid of heights. I remembered all that I was learning on this trip and decided to just go for it. For every question, I just answered "Chicken" and we went forward.

At 5:55 p.m. we reached the top, and they all said, "Are you ready?" I said, "Yes." We crested the top and headed deep into the valley. I heard a new voice say, "Welcome home!" We began to pass what seemed like millions of people along the roadway in this lush, technicolored garden. All the people had shining eyes and were waving and saying, "Welcome back!" and "Glad you decided to return!" For some strange reason, I remembered them all as if I had been gone for only a short while in some bad dream. Now I was home again and I couldn't wait to see them all again. At this time, I heard one of the angels say, "He's remembering." I was glad to be home.

Heaven was so beautiful. It was as if all the colors on earth are in black and white, but in heaven they vibrate. They are alive. I quickly realized that heaven is where those lush scents were coming from. The closer I got, the more potent the aroma became. I had this incredible vibration all over my body and finally *knew* what it felt like to be alive. All the vegetation I encountered was alive and had many ancient stories to tell.

I learned a great appreciation for all living things there. There were a great many things I learned in heaven, but one thing that became apparent was that they expected me to return of my own free will. They said that it would be best since I had much to return to. I didn't know what they meant, but I agreed. After a final question and answer session, they promised that I would return when I was through with travels on the earth. They then asked me, "Where is heaven?" I answered, "Heaven is where you find it." They once again shook their heads, "*No.*"

There were a great many things that I learned in heaven, many of which I cannot share at this time. Given all the time I spent there, it seemed like a million years. It was made clear to me that they controlled everything. Upon my return, it would be as if three days had passed. I was amazed, but after seeing all that was shown to me, I no longer doubted anything. I told them I knew they had to erase a great portion of this event, but to at least leave me with some of it. They assured me they would and they left me to be alone for a while.

I remember talking to a tree. The things it had to tell I understood *in exotic and tasty scents that my soul recognized*. I once again felt really old. I remember asking the sky where I was and it answered, "Third Heaven." I asked if I could see God and they said that everyone would see God at the same time. I then asked if I could see Jesus and they said I would.

I remember feeling *overwhelmed and complete*. Then the three beings returned and led me to a bedroom where I fell asleep. There were many places I experienced while I slept, but due to my decision to return, all memory of them has been erased. I do remember being in awe.

On Saturday, February 20, I remember being awakened by a shimmery figure out of the corner of my eye. When I finally focused, I realized it was Jesus. I was immediately overwhelmed by love. I remember feeling like a child who could just could soak up that love forever. Once again, I was given a review of my life. This time, the thing I was made the most aware of was that, all my life, Jesus was always there. From an early age, I was taught this but being in the presence of Jesus, I really felt it. We conversed for what seemed to be a long time. I remember thinking that out of everything in heaven, talking this candidly with Jesus was what I would miss the most.

He then said He was glad that I decided to return and wished me luck and peace on my return. He asked me, "So, Andre, where is heaven?" This time I replied, *"Heaven is inside of you."* He smiled and said, "Go, be on your way." I remember feeling proud that Jesus believed in me enough to allow me to return to earth. Just before Jesus left, He pointed at me and I felt my wounded side heal. This truly amazed me, and I remember saying to myself that I was ready to go back. I drifted back to sleep.

I awoke once again feeling invigorated. The three beings once again came to me and we conversed. They understood that I really wanted to return and begin to make some sense of my life. They wanted to wish me well. I wanted to know how it would happen and they said, "You'll see."

Saturday, February 20, 1:11 p.m. On the ride back home, it sort of reversed itself. We headed back and it seemed like the heavenly scent was the first to go. Then that incredible all-knowing feeling went away. The closer we got to Vallejo where I lived, the more the vibrations slowed down. And, as if in big farewell, all three of the angels said goodbye just before leaving Julie, Renee and Robert's eyes. It sounds strange, but in reflection, I understand it—more now than then.

Just like that, they were gone. One moment I was in heaven and the next I was on a gravel highway headed toward Vallejo. I felt my side and it felt great. I was happy to be alive, happy and grateful to have experienced such an adventure. To this day, I could never truly describe it with three-dimensional words. But no matter what, I would not forget my adventures in wonderland. The real gift was that I now had plenty of time to change my life if I wanted to. And I wanted to. . . I *wanted* to.

In the months that followed my death experience, I eventually split for good from my 11-year relationship. We remain good friends to this very day. I realized after this experience that we were not in love. I also realized that it was all right to demand more out of life. I set about making some extreme changes over the next few years.

This experience created a profound and positive effect that continues to blossom over the years. I have had many other adventures, but none quite as profound as this one. Later, I would meet and fall in love with the man that I am currently in love with. He is someone I not only love, but also respect and with whom I have a great friendship that has blossomed over the years—my lover Russell.

1. Did sexual identity come into play during your NDE?

Yes (see story). I said it was all right and the joke was on people who thought that it wasn't.

2. After the NDE, did the near-death experience change your sexual identify in any way or change the way you feel about your sexual identity?

Yes, I became more free and more open with my identity. In fact, it was possible to have a much deeper relationship that meant something—even more so than the prior one.

An NDE by Drowning as a Child

Joan is a doctor of chiropractic working in a group of natural healthcare practitioners, the Labrys Healthcare Circle. As a board member of the non-profit Associates for Community Education, she is the founder of the Labrys School of Self-Healing Arts for Wimmin and Girls, publishes a newsletter for holistic healing and is a founding member of the East Bay Women's Building. At age 57, she loves living with cats, singing, playing recorders and sailing on San Francisco Bay.

All of us in our swim suits with towels draped around our necks—my cousins, my brother, my father, and myself—walked among the huge redwood trees from my grandparents' cabin in Paradise Park. We passed the covered bridge on our way to Sandy Beach, our favorite on the San Lorenzo River near Santa Cruz.

As we arrived, I spied a big inner tube I wanted to play on and ran to it. At the same time I got there, so did another little girl about my same age of four. We agreed to play together, dragged the tube into the water and got on. As we faced each other with each sitting on one side of the tube, the water was only up to our ankles. Gently we floated a bit downstream away from the beach.

We talked about how it might be dangerous if the tube drifted into deep water and that we wanted to stay near the reeds by the shore. I got the bright idea that I could dangle off the tube to find out if I could still touch bottom. Then we would know if it was too deep.

Hugging the top of the tube, I slipped into the water, my toes reaching for the mud. Maybe water splashed onto the tube. For whatever reason, my hands slipped and into the water I fell.

I do not remember struggling or being afraid. I felt only deep peace and happiness. While my body was at the bottom of the river, I remember looking up toward the surface. I enjoyed watching a beautiful array of dancing, brilliant sparkles of color from the yellow sunlight coming through the river water. I was calm and fascinated by the beauty of the light and the reeds coming out of the mud. I also remember being wonderfully happy, peaceful and excited at the same time. I stayed there in this bliss for a very long time.

The scene changed. I looked around me and noticed some treetops nearby. My eyes followed the trees down to the ground, and I realized with a shock that I was up here in the air, way above the ground. I turned around and looked across the river at the trees on the other side. I recognized the tree that holds the rope swing. I remember thinking, "My boy cousins use it all the time, swing out over the river and drop into the water. But I'm not big enough yet."

My eyes crossed the river again. As I looked down at the sandy beach below me, I saw kids running toward a group in the center. I wondered what they were all clustered around on the sand, but could not see through them. I stayed watching them for a long time, wondering what they found so interesting there.

Suddenly, I was surprised to find what they were looking at: Me! I was looking up at a ring of faces. I felt an intense desire that I live and be well. Fifty years later, I realized it was probably my brother's and my father's feelings, not my own, because in my memory I had no desire except to see why the crowd had gathered. It was my dad who had been pushing rhythmically on my back and pulling up on my arms in the 1940's style of resuscitation.

I felt excited and happy about this adventure. When we returned to the cabin, my grandparents scolded and blamed me for the mishap. Their reaction frightened me, creating an intense fear of them that I associated with the drowning.

My mother, who was not present that weekend, but was home in the East Bay Area, pulled a few pieces of the story from me. It took her a week to drag out enough pieces to get a skimpy picture. My father denied to her that anything out of the ordinary had happened, and he still denies it to this day. Although I felt that I could not tell anyone about the drowning and near-death experience (NDE), I held its memory in my heart as a treasure.

My mother immediately got me into swimming lessons, which I remember vividly. At first I screamed in fear. I am sure my reaction was not to the water itself, nor to the idea of death, but to my grandparents' reaction to the near-drowning. Because of my mother's quick action, I got over my "fear of water," though not of my grandparents. In hindsight I realize they were two people I never loved. As a child I felt my mother's total support for my, as yet, locked-away story. Throughout my childhood, I loved swimming. I remember teaching myself how to dive backward.

I may have had another near-death experience (NDE) at birth from a forceps delivery. Who knows what procedures may have been used to "fix" the problem, but ten days later when my mother first saw me, the signs of a brain concussion were evident. What were my feelings during those first days of my life? Angry? Afraid? Wanting my mommy? I have neither memories nor dreams I attribute to my birth trauma.

There is no way of knowing for sure which aspects of my personality, emotions, and mental functioning were the effects of NDE, because I was so young when I drowned. I have no sense of "before" or "after." However, about every two years throughout my childhood, I had short blackouts with total loss of consciousness and motor nerve control. Unless I found myself somewhere I did not expect, like fallen at the bottom of a staircase, I did not know I had gone out or lost consciousness. It is my intuitive sense that these blackouts, or "going out" of my physical body are related to the NDE.

In my early twenties, I lived in Bolivia for two years as a Peace Corps Volunteer. I taught health and hygiene in several grammar schools and wrote a how-to book in Spanish for Bolivian teachers. While there I had a blackout while rock climbing. After saving myself, I rescued my companion who was frozen in fear on a cliff face. What she calls super-human strength and extreme "bravery" I would call fearlessness.

Beginning in my early twenties, the car crashes began: 17 to date. Of course, I wondered if I could have prevented the crashes. Was I distracted or sleepy or careless? Both the car insurance company and I never found them to be my fault. I never suspected that I was repeatedly having blackouts. So I took classes in defensive driving.

Parts of my story may not be related to the NDE. In my early teens, I experienced emotional burnout from all the family stress of my parents' 50s style divorce. I battled depression between the ages of 14 and 23 and was suicidal. What I most remember feeling was that I wanted to not be here. Was my subconscious wanting to go to out-of-body again to find bliss?

Until my late twenties, I was aware of a black hole in my center, never telling anyone about it until my fifties. Whenever I would become aware of it, I felt great fear. Now I believe that the black hole was near-death, which for me has been the most beautiful and peaceful experience in my life. The fear I felt upon becoming aware of the blackness in me was the fear of my grandparents and their reaction to my drowning. I had been frightened by them into never telling anyone of the beauty, peace, happiness, and truth I had known. Although my father denied my experience, I knew it was true. I symbolized my spirit's experience with blackness, while I repeated my body's experience with fear.

At age 34, I came out as a lesbian, a strong amazon wielding a double edged ax, a labrys. I wanted to wipe out the heteropatriarchy and establish safety for all women in societies all over the world.

That same year my Kaiser (an HMO) doctor found I had a pre-cancerous condition of the cervix, but when I asked him questions about it, he got angry at me. So I fired him and Kaiser. I set myself the task of answering my own questions, like, "How can I prevent cancer?" I moved to Ohio to live near an excellent homeopathic doctor who monitored my condition. After a couple of years, when I was 37, she found it had progressed to cancer. With her help I healed myself without drugs or surgery by using a homeopathic remedy and by improving my nutrition. (For those homeopaths among my readers, I believe carcinogen is my constitutional remedy.)

In the 1970s, there were few female or holistic doctors available. I figured that as a middle-class white woman and a feminist I had a responsibility to help all women improve our health. I was learning how to use herbs, foods, and homeopathy to promote my own well-being. I realized I would have more influence in others' lives if I changed careers from journalism to health care. Also, I knew that if I went to medical school, neither I nor the professors would survive my rage at the rampant sexism.

By way of selecting my next path, I looked at the people in various health care professions. I talked with nurses, osteopaths, naturopaths, acupuncturists, even dentists as health care professionals who could teach me. I chose chiropractic because of its emphasis on the nervous system and its effect on the immune system. Also, I liked the chiropractors I met and I appreciated that chiropractic allows the body to heal itself without drugs and surgery. I particularly resonated with chiropractors who use muscle testing as a part of their methods of diagnosis, Applied Kinesiologists, and decided to become an AK doctor.

During the several years I was recovering from cancer, I began studying to go to chiropractic college. My goal of becoming a healer was an important part of my recovery. I graduated eight years later and opened my practice in Oakland, California.

Returning to the San Francisco Bay Area after eleven years away was wonderful for me; I was coming home. Something I noticed this time and had not before was that whenever I look at the Bay, I sigh. And when I sigh, I feel a deep peace and I smile. Perhaps this is the black hole without the fear? The same sigh happens when I look at the ocean. Ah, deep water: this is the source of my most beautiful experience in fifty-seven years. It's no wonder that sailing is a favorite recreation for me.

It was not until my fifties that I had a revealing incident while treating a patient's spine. She was face down on the treatment table and I had just checked her leg length at the foot of the table. I stepped to the right and took a step on my way toward the head of the table. With no warning my knees bent almost to the ground as all my postural muscles turned off for a split second and my vision dimmed. I had started to go out mid-stride and then returned mid-fall. There were no symptoms afterwards and I kept working without skipping a beat. Not even my patient noticed. This incident occurred during a period of two years during which I had six car crashes. I finally got it. The blackouts I had thought had stopped in my 20s were still with me, though shorter. Very scary!

I quickly changed my assumption of "no fault" and took myself to a medical neurologist for a neurological work-up. When the results revealed nothing, he told me to "pay better attention while driving." In search of a more adequate solution, I made two important steps toward taking control.

Being a chiropractic physician myself, I focused on a new specialty, chiropractic neurology, which is being developed by Ted Carrick, DC. In tapes of his lectures he describes amazing success in bringing patients out of comas and other brain dysfunctions. So I found a chiropractic neurologist who practices Carrick's work. He was able to analyze my brain function and give me very specific spinal adjustments. As a result the quality of my consciousness on all levels improved, as have the neurological results on follow-up examinations.

Within months of beginning care with the chiropractic neurologist, I found Diana Schmidt's NDE support group in El Cerrito, California. She told me to read Phyllis Atwater's

Beyond the Light. This support felt like coming home to myself. I had the pleasure of meeting Ms. Atwater and reading another of her books, *Future Memory.* In this book, Ms. Atwater "attempts to describe the indescribable—that moment of brain shift after a spiritual transformation when realities switch and new ways of perceiving existence replace former beliefs." I could relate fully.

Some of the common characteristics Ms. Atwater has found among people with NDEs immediately rang bells for me. Naiveté, a childlike trust, openness to psychic phenomenon and fearlessness fit me perfectly. Except for fearing my grandparents and that black hole in my center, I did not really know fear as other people describe it. For instance, while rock climbing, sailing, swimming, hitchhiking, riding the rails and climbing mountains, I always take unnecessary risks without fear, knowing all will be well.

Being a risk-taker plus my flexibility and creativity have enabled me to succeed in many areas. As an example, I decided to go to Alaska the summer I was 21 to seek my fortune so as to pay for college. I asked a friend to go with me and we costumed ourselves at the local war surplus store to pass as boys. Then we hopped a freight train out of the Oakland yards and had many adventures along the way. We arrived safely in Cordova, Alaska, having hitchhiked by boat, truck, and airplane as well as by rail, and were arrested only once for trespassing.

I got jobs in the salmon and crab canneries and was making big bucks by working 14 to 16 hour days. However, I had not counted on the high cost of imported food that ate up most of my wages. We lived in an abandoned cannery up the coast, two young women with some fishermen, and walked to work through the forest, meeting bears at our and their favorite breakfast blackberry patches. In hindsight, every difficulty I encountered that summer I solved by youthful optimism and creativity. To get there at all, I had been fearless, taking risks and completely trusting strangers, including wild animals.

Among my physical characteristics in common with other people with NDEs are low blood pressure and pulse rate. I have always looked and acted younger than my age. I cannot tolerate loud sounds and am sensitive to noise. I forgo pharmaceuticals in favor of homeopathy, herbs, and other healing alternatives. I prefer open doors and windows and seldom use curtains or shades. I am able to merge into things easily, and attract animals and birds to me.

Also, I have a heightened awareness of the present moment, which means I am never bored. Either I have developed healing hands in my work, or I went into chiropractic intuitively knowing I have healing hands. I occasionally see ghosts or beings not present physically. And I have occasionally known the future before it happens, or have had future memory. Whole scenes of action appear to me superimposed on top of present reality, and I learn that what I "saw" actually happened later.

Ms. Atwater's research has found some of my own characteristics to be unusual physiological aftereffects of

NDE. In ten years of practice, I have been a gifted healer. I find I have psychokinetic abilities to use my mind to move matter, particularly spinal vertebrae. My empathetic abilities make me a focused, caring listener for my patients and friends.

Another of my characteristics which Ms. Atwater verified for me as an effect of NDE is my discomfort in being around electronic devices. I reject wearing a watch, I am not comfortable around computers and microwave ovens and I do not watch television. Research has found that the electromagnetic fields that surround the average person are different from those of people with NDE.

Furthermore, I am determined to make a difference in the world and to help others, hence joining the Peace Corps and later becoming a doctor. I tend to have grandiose dreams that I cannot explain to others. Heteropatriarchial codes of conduct lose relevance as vast areas of interest and inquiry take priority. As a teenager, I had great difficulty with communication and therefore became a journalist, learning to talk again by producing feminist radio programs at KPFA. In my relationships I am not demanding or jealous because I love and accept others' differences without being possessive. All my life I have felt I am dancing to a tune no one else can hear. These are all psychological aftereffects of NDE explained in detail in *Beyond the Light*.

Through extensive research with many people who have had a brain shift following an NDE (turbulent method) or in conjunction with spiritual disciplines (tranquil method), Ms.

Atwater found that they may have significant restructuring of brain function. They "display a childlike innocence and simplicity, along with an increase in intelligence." It rings true with me, for I am always asking curious questions, always asking WHY? A friend describes me as never letting boxes limit me, having a constant freshness, always being open to new ideas and always in wonder at the world, like a kid.

A perfect daily example is my passion for my work as an Applied Kinesiologist and chiropractor. To give some background information, I digress from my NDE story for a few paragraphs.

In my bones I know that by using muscle testing and intuition to help me diagnose a patient's health problems, I am speaking with spirit, my own in communication with my patient's. This is the same spirit that is called *qi* or *chi* by the Chinese, *prana* in the yogi traditions of India and Tibet and *orenda* by the Iroquois, to name but a few of the more than four hundred different names used to describe spirit in cultures all over the world.

In the Chinese view of health, *chi* flows in meridians or channels throughout the body. By using acupuncture or acupressure a practitioner finds areas where the *chi* is stuck and unblocks it, allowing the spirit to flow freely again. In the yogi tradition *prana* spins in vortices created within us by the interpenetration of spirit and the physical body. These energy vortices are located in front of the spine, in line with the spinal cord and brain. The great success of chiropractic adjustments these last hundred years is due to stimulation of the meridians and vortices of spirit, which chiropractors call innate intelligence.

At the beginning of each office visit, my patient lists her many health complaints. Then we explore together, looking for the underlying reasons for the symptoms. An investigative journalist for 20 years, I have become a health sleuth.

As an AK doctor I combine muscle testing and a Western doctor's knowledge of the physical body with challenges to the acupuncture meridians, the chakras, and other energy structures, such as neurolymphatic and neruovascular points. While working with each patient I muscle test and make note of the muscles that test strong and those that test weak. (On a scale of zero to five, zero represents total paralysis, a four is weak and five is perfect neurological function.) Applied Kinesiologists associate each muscle with a meridian and with a gland or organ. For instance, I associate the latissimus dorsi muscle in the back with the spleen meridian and the pancreas gland.

Then I challenge mostly the patient's physical body, but also her etheric, astral, mental, and other spiritual bodies by any of hundreds of challenges. I may use touch, taste, thought, sound, emotion, hot, cold or stress, individual foods or their basic nutrients. I am looking for a change in muscle strength, indicating an underlying contributing cause of the symptoms. Whenever I find something that I feel is working less than perfectly, I explain to my patient what I have found, using Western health care language so I will not appear too weird. I use gentle chiropractic adjustments, called Network

Chiropractic, nutrition with food or herbs and meridian therapy, using a laser instead of needles.

By retesting the muscles with the same challenges that had previously caused a change in muscle strength, I demonstrate that both the muscle and the associated gland or organ function are now improved. The patient gets some homework to help maintain the adjustments. Invariably the work finds us laughing a lot, excited by the discoveries we make. My work makes me very happy, and I have a lot of fun. It's a lot like the fun and excitement I had as a kid.

An important clue to my NDE puzzle happens when I am treating a patient, with my fingers on the place where the energy is stuck. An acupuncture meridian may be blocked in its normal flow of *chi* or a spinal vertebra may be limited in its normal range of movement, thereby blocking nervous energy. Or when I focus on a particular chakra in, let's say, the etheric body, I will find a vertebral subluxation (lack of normal movement) where previously there was none physically.

When the energy moves, I sigh or yawn. If I get impatient and retest the stuck place before I have sighed, I usually find it is still stuck. The sigh or yawn happens with a release of stuck energy, either the patient's or mine. Sometimes both the patient and I sigh together. Also, for weeks or months after a car crash, depending on the severity of the violence to my body, I do not sigh when looking at the Bay or working with patients.

I remember that as an early teen my mother took me to see a Kaiser doctor complaining that I had begun to sigh a lot. This is when I believe my sensitivity to the release of energy began, with my female hormonal changes. I did not notice as a young adult that my sighs coincided with any particular emotion or situation.

Another important clue to what I experience when I focus on a patient's body comes from Phyllis Atwater's *Future Memory*:

> "What (Australian aborigines) call 'dreaming' has little to do with sleep or dreams which occur during sleep. Dreaming for them is actually more akin to a type of 'flow' in which one *becomes* whatever one focused upon and suddenly knows whatever needs to be known at the moment. . . In this state of consciousness, participants seem to 'merge with' or 'enter into' soil, rocks, animals, sky, or whatever else they focus on including the 'In-between' (that which appears to exist between time and space, as if through a crack in creation)."

When I am totally focused on a patient's spine with my fingers on her physical body, I often feel in my own body where her energy is blocked and "see" through the skin to her vertebrae or nerve root that has been compromised by the energy blockage. It comes from practicing muscle testing and chiropractic for so many years and learning (even in this science-driven field of health care) to trust this new perspective on reality. Again, it has to do with childlike trust. And it has to do with having seen life after death as a child.

Unfortunately, the accidents resumed recently, four within seven months in 1998, following a two-year period of none. For the first accident, I was not even in the car. I had parked it next to Lake Merritt in Oakland and a speeding driver ran into it. When I returned and found it gone, a waiting cop with the culprit in his squad car told me how it was totally demolished and towed.

A few months later while dancing I stepped back onto a water bottle, slipped and fell backward. I sailed about ten feet over several chairs, out an open door onto the deck and landed on my back and head, my feet above me on the porch railing. Luckily I am a chiropractor and could immediately begin self-treatments.

I was injured in two car crashes and neither involved "going out." In August, I pulled into the right lane on a city street next to a long, semi truck. When I was almost past it, right next to the front wheel, the driver pulled into my lane, hitting me five times as it went by, once with each set of wheels. He apologized for neither looking nor signaling and his passenger agreed the accident was clearly the trucker's fault.

In November I stopped for a pedestrian in a cross walk and the car behind me did not. Again, I assumed that another driver was a safe driver. He was not and hit me at full speed.

What is my task now? In addition to maintaining my mental and physical health as best I can through top-notch chiropractic care, I must ask, "How can I prevent accidents?" The answers that come to me are not physical but spiritual.

Recently I gained a new perspective by consulting a feminist astrologer. She was shocked to see in my natal chart "a huge pileup in the eighth house," four planets, including both Saturn, guardian of the old patriarchal order, and Uranus, the planet of revolution against all oppressions. Their being in the eighth house, she told me, indicates that in this life I would experience death, disease and loss of control, all of which feed my spiritual purpose of shamanism—to be a healer and teacher. She's right: death by drowning, disease by cancer, and loss of control in accidents help me to be a better doctor.

I now believe seventeen car crashes is the limit, because since that last one, I have twice again encountered the number 17. Both instances have to do with the *Nambudripad Allergy Elimination Technique* (NAET) which is an essential part of my practice.

During the last five years, the most intense period of car crashes, I have gradually changed the way in which I practice NAET, adding more and more challenges as a part of muscle testing my patients' nervous systems. Every time I created a new challenge, I felt I had to retest my previous work on every patient. There were three such additions this year alone, and I was over-working myself every patient visit, so as to try and keep up with my original treatment plan. I was exhausted at the end of each workday with patients. I cried out to the goddesses to stop these additional challenges that I felt driven to add to the original NAET technique. And then I did something I'd never done before—I listed them all and then counted them—seventeen.

While I was attending an advanced class in NAET a few months later, Dr. Devi Nambudripad, originator of the technique, admonished those of us who had diverted energy away from the basics of the technique by adding many extra challenges, exactly what I had been doing. She stopped me at seventeen.

Later that same day, she told us of a family celebration when they chose to go to Las Vegas. Although she herself doesn't like to gamble, she agreed to go along with the plan. But instead of letting her spend an afternoon leisurely reading a book, they insisted that she sit down at a slot machine and gamble. To please them, she put a quarter in the machine and she won. She changed machines and she won again. So she moved to another machine, and she won again and again and again. Finally, her family members all around her cheering, she said, "That's enough," and she stopped, at seventeen wins.

All three appearances of seventeen were circumstances of saying, "No More! Stop!" My body conscious mind learned that the seventeenth crash was one of the experiences I needed to learn that the accidents stop here. Interestingly, $1 + 7 = 8$, relating the seventeen car crashes to my eighth house pileup of planets.

1. Did sexual identity come into play during your NDE?

No.

2. After the NDE, did the near-death experience change your sexual identify in any way or change the way you feel about your sexual identity?

No.

SOULFUL GROWTH

Author is a writer, international business consultant, hospice volunteer and Reiki practitioner.

My NDE-like experience was a climax of spiritual experiences which began three years earlier with my mother's death. That day, After Death Communication (ADC), seeing and telepathically talking to my mother's spirit the night of her death and at her funeral, being awestruck by her sugar crystal gown and shimmering rainbow radiance, and "knowing" there is a soul, an afterlife and a creator—at a cellular level, several transformations began. Soon after, I began seeing flashes and sparks of light, some visions and ESP, bought my first book on spirituality (Scott Peck's *The Road Less Traveled* —read it six times), began to meditate, and went to church for the first time in over twelve years, a Unitarian Church one block away. More intense feelings and cravings for soulful growth and reflection continued, and escalated, for three years. Yet, still rather "low-keyed," as Scott Peck claimed in *The Road*.

I was <u>not</u> prepared for the NDE-like experience: it was shocking and dramatic to mind, body, and soul. Nothing "low-key" about it. It was overwhelming and ineffable: I was reeling from it for weeks, and some aspects, for months. It has taken many years to absorb it into my life—mind, body, and soul levels.

It is the most important, stunningly exquisite event in my life: basking in the light, experiencing our creator's love, power, and majesty are beyond description. Divine ecstasy and intoxication is about as close as I can begin to "translate" this into human words.

Alice Walker's remark "Everything comes from the silence" was indeed true for me, for that was the "triggering" event which prompted my NDE-like experience. I was lounging quietly, innocently on my living room couch, half meditating and half napping—that's how it started. Then I noticed with half closed, glazed eyes, a glowing light moving toward and through my sliding glass doors into the living room. I first thought it was the sun doing some weird reflections, then I saw that it was vibrant, "alive," and moving about, changing form and shape—enveloping more and more of the room, and eventually me. I stood up to investigate, going toward the window through which it had entered. Then I was totally enveloped by and merged with the light—undulating and basking in and with the intoxicating, saturating love of the divine being. The experience was so deep, intense, and powerful I crumpled to my knees, then fell on the floor, with tears of joy in my eyes. My body/spirit could not handle any more of this overpowering immersion:

> It was like a 220 volt current frazzling a 110 volt socket. It almost became unbearable: the huge wave after wave of exquisite joy, communion, presence of the divine fused with a limited human being....

I was told, "You're going home..." I had no way to ask or to respond to what that meant; I was reeling with the experience. Yet I "knew" it was my *real* home, not here.

Then I "saw" or experienced a T-square fountain of bubbles, greyish tinged yet translucent. The flow of bubbles kept pouring forth in a playful, frothing manner. There were things, scenes, people, movement in each one of the bubbles; I couldn't see the details. I knew I was connected to the bubbles, and that they held important information/meanings.

Then I began to expand myself and "disperse" into small particles and merge into the nearby stone fireplace, outdoor trees, the very molecules of CO_2 in the air, and to wisps and undulating "seasons" of infinity that swirled around me. It was as if I was being made to "know" the universe and unity of all existence, on earth and of other realms by being bathed and linked with divine grace, power, and love.

Finally it all ended and dissolved in a very gentle manner, slipping away and disappearing with a "soft landing," so to speak. However, I was still sprawled on the floor, a pile of molecular mush: I could barely move, had tears in my eyes, and struggled to get up. My head and body still danced with dazzle and tingled with flooded, overloaded "circuits." I was reeling as I walked a few steps, still absorbing the intoxicating energies and soul transforming experience with the divine light. I knew that my mind, body, and soul were launched to a new realm of perception and being. Irreversible changes.

I lost six pounds in two weeks after the experience: I could barely eat. Spontaneous tears of joy and some flashbacks or residual aftermath feelings also saturated my awareness in the first few weeks. Time warped in, out, around, and about in dizzying varieties of manifestations. It was difficult to stay "grounded" and to carry on routine daily life and work schedules.

Over the next several months, another cycle of spiritual phenomena unfolded: Kundalini and Chakra experiences exploding forth (thankfully all positive and "manageable," considering the intensity of what is unleashed). I had no idea what was happening to me, being unaware of the concept Kundalini; out-of-body experiences (OBEs); automatic writing; dreams and visions; telepathy/ESP/premonitions; seeing sparks of colors and lights; cravings for using my left hand; seeing auras around people; cravings to read quantum physics and spiritual books on all varieties of topics; "knowing" intuitively others' feelings and thoughts; "knowing" my various life missions; "knowing" that reincarnation is true, not a flight of fancy for daydreamers/fools; joining Unity Church and prayer groups; studying healing practices and becoming a Reiki Level II; studying death and dying and becoming a Hospice volunteer, etc.

My spiritual and personal development during the years since my experience has been my top priority. Learning about our divine dialogue and personal relationship is a key commitment and focus. We are here on this earth to celebrate life, to love and help one another, and to tap into and use all the gifts and talents our creator has endowed us with, i.e. pursuing our "mission" on earth within the divine plan. Unconditional love applied on a daily basis is how we help ourselves to evolve, and touch other people's lives. Giving and receiving are fused together. We each have our own unique path, yet we all are on the same journey: "conforming to the Creator's likeness, day by day..." and finally—"going home..."

It takes many years to incorporate all the dynamics and impact of NDE into your life (PMH Atwater was right!). Practicing unconditional love, giving and receiving, etc., is a daily and lifelong experiential lesson/gift.

INTER-
CONNECTEDNESS

Steve is a well-known photographer in San Francisco. His work has appeared in most major gay periodicals regularly over the past 25 years, his portraits have adorned the jackets of over a dozen books, and his performing-arts photographs appear almost daily in the newspapers and magazines of the San Francisco Bay Area.

My near-death experience began around 9 o'clock on the night of October 2, 1996, at a large San Francisco medical center where I had been operated on two days before to have an infected prosthesis removed from my shoulder. I had entered the hospital with considerable anxiety, since I had had four previous surgeries on this same shoulder. Each time, I came out of the hospital a little more disabled—with a little more limited use of my left arm. My assistant, and dear friend, Edel, had dropped me off at the hospital on Monday morning, and the operation started around noon. It was a fairly lengthy procedure. Just now—in April, 1997—I have had a chance to read the operative report. They had to pry and chisel and saw to get the damned thing out, all the while trying to preserve the dense network of muscles and nerves surrounding the humeral head (the prosthesis itself had replaced the head of my humerus bone which had been shattered in a bicycle accident a year earlier). I awoke at about 4:00 p.m. in the recovery area, and was in a hospital room on the sixth floor by 4:30 p.m.

My former physical therapist, Sal, was the first person to call to see how I was doing. Of course, at that point, I hardly knew myself. A little later, Edel called to see if I had survived the operation. And in the early evening, my friend Tina called to say she would be in the next day to see me, and did I want any food? During a previous hospital stay, she had brought sushi to my bedside. I slept poorly that first night. I had taken a four hour "nap" during the operation, but awoke early the next morning feeling pretty good. I was relieved to have the operation over with. I had struggled for two months with the decision about whether to have the prosthesis removed, with the attendant risk of complete disability, or to live the rest of my life on antibiotics to keep the infection under control. That day, Tuesday, I had many visitors. My friends Tina, Robert, Bill, Sal, and Edel all stopped by for brief visits. Around four in the afternoon, when Tina, Robert and Sal were all there together, a nurse came in and said she had been ordered to install a Landmark IV in my right arm. I knew I was to have six weeks of intravenous antibiotics after surgery. This was how they were to be administered: a Landmark is a fairly rigid plastic tube with a point on one end which is threaded into a vein so that the antibiotics can be administered intramuscularly. In this way, they are less likely to cause irritation and medication will be dispersed through the body more quickly.

The nurse who had been assigned to install my Landmark was a sweet Asian girl, Miyoko, who said she didn't mind if my visitors stayed while she slipped the thing into my arm. As for me, I was glad to have the distraction of my friends around me during the rather grisly procedure—I never watch the needle going in when I have shots or when they draw blood—and this was, in effect, an eight-inch needle. Poor Miyoko seemed to have a few problems finding the appropriate vein—she tapped and squeezed and prodded the inside of my elbow until she was satisfied that the vein was sufficiently juicy and firm to sustain the Landmark. While Robert told me funny stories, and Sal made faces, she poked the sharp tip into my arm. She pushed and pushed until it nestled deep in my upper arm. But for some reason, it bent when it hit the side of the vein near my biceps. So, she pulled it out and unwrapped a fresh one. Again, she threaded the thing into my arm while Robert joked and Sal grimaced and Tina looked away. And again, the damned thing hit a muscle and was bent. She tried a third time. Finally, it seemed to go in successfully. Another nurse primed it with saline solution and then switched the IV-line, which had been going into my forearm, to the new Landmark. I was all set for the next six weeks. Or so we all thought.

That night, October 1, I slept badly again. I was too excited by all the visitors, and by the constant droning voice coming from the wife of my roommate—an elderly man who had had a tumor the size of a grapefruit removed from his abdomen. The wife was by his side from 8:00 in the morning until 10:00 at night that day.

Sweet and considerate as she was, she began to get on my nerves. Around midnight when the new shift came on, I rang for the nurse and asked for a sleeping pill. The night nurse, Susan, was warm and friendly, in sharp contrast to the harried and overworked staff during the day. She said I shouldn't feel badly about needing a pill to get to sleep, and did I want any more morphine for the pain? Actually, the pain had not been all that bad this time around. Monday night, I had availed myself of the regular morphine shots (every 2 hours). By Tuesday, I felt well enough to forego the morphine and to rely on codeine. Codeine is administered in the form of tablets and is therefore much easier for the nursing staff to dispense. With the sleeping pill, I slept pretty well that night, and woke up to a hearty breakfast. It generally takes about 24 hours in a hospital to train the dietitian. For example, I don't eat meat, and I love all those heavy breakfast foods like pancakes, French toast, and oatmeal. Generally, other patients can't handle these foods.

Wednesday was a pretty quiet day. My surgeon, Dr. Thomas, came by to see how I was doing. My infectious disease specialist, Dr. Stephens, accompanied him. By now, of course, everyone knew what was covered by insurance and what was not, so there was no longer any delay with getting painkillers, physical therapy, a social worker, etc. That afternoon, my friend Paul came by for an extended visit. My German teacher, Hans, brought flowers and tried to give me my lesson in the hospital. Later in the day, my assistants, Edel and Regina, stopped by and after them, Peter, my former assistant. It was lovely seeing them all, but by supper time, I was tired and a little groggy. As a hospital veteran, I had arranged to have a VCR brought to the room, and my friend Paul had brought some videos for me to watch. I started watching *The Seagull,* the marvelous movie of the Chekhov play, with James Mason and Vanessa Redgrave, around 8:00. I had watched about half of it when I began to feel slightly light-headed. It felt as though caffeine were being infused through the Landmark. My mind began racing. My heart-rate accelerated. I began to sweat, and then to feel chilly, as my blood pressure fluctuated. I began to see flashes of various periods of my life: my mother when I was a young child, friends from high school, my assistant Edel from earlier that same evening. I could feel my heart throbbing in my chest. I looked at my watch for a moment to time my heartbeat, and noticed that the seconds were passing incredibly slowly—

one, two, three heartbeats per second. I began to hear sounds and to smell odd aromas, and the flashes of past experiences continued and became more vivid. Now I was actually *experiencing scenes* from earlier life, not just the sight of them, but the sound, the smells, the tactile impressions, the heat and the cold, and even the emotions that were associated with each one. I thought to myself, "I must be dying." I wondered exactly how I should face my own death.

At first, I felt anger at the hospital, and especially at Miyoko, the IV nurse. I thought of calling my friend Robert (who had witnessed the clumsy installation of the Landmark). I wanted to make sure he sued the hospital so that at least my heirs would get some money out of this thing. But this thought of vengeance quickly dissolved as the barrage of sense impressions—the smells, the sounds, the pictures, all of it—continued to cascade through my brain. It was like a waterfall rushing through my mind. I had determined by this time that the IV was somehow causing what was happening to me. I called the overworked evening nurse to come and take a look. She proclaimed herself helpless to evaluate what was going on other than to confirm my rapid heart rate, my elevated blood pressure and a slight fever. She summoned a special evening IV nurse. She took one look at my arm and saw that it was swelling and turning red in blotches where the end of the IV hit the muscle of my arm. It had pierced through the wall of the vein, and was infusing antibiotics, and the chemicals used to disperse them, into my biceps. This caused a rapid onset of phlebitis, a relatively serious condition which can cause blood clotting, and secondary strokes or heart attacks as the clot travels in the vein to the heart or lungs. She immediately summoned an emergency nurse to pull the IV and replace it with a conventional one while slapping my arm in an effort to relieve the swelling and to break up the blood-clots.

Meanwhile, the sensory kaleidoscope continued inside my head. I was only dimly aware of all the nurses rushing in and out, the slapping of my arm and upper body, the pounding of my chest, the actual pulling of the IV, etc. I was lost in a world of brilliant images from my past: all my friends, my relatives, and even childhood friends—everyone was gathering around me at my bedside. My thoughts of vengeance toward the hospital gave way to the thought that I did not want to leave this world with such negative energy consuming my consciousness. I thought of my friend Edel. I thought that if I were really to die, I needed to call him to tell him how much I cared about him. I needed to leave this life with words of love on my lips and in my ear. I reached for the phone, clumsily, with my post-operative left arm, as nurses flailed around my right arm. I managed to get the phone onto my chest, ready, in case I should need it, despite the frantic activity around me.

Somehow the thought of Edel and my feelings for him and for the other friends gathering around me, transformed the experience I was having. The waterfall of sensation and emotion began to narrow into a single stream, flowing into a brightly-lit meadow. It became narrower still, until it was thread-like—just a single strand of feeling and sensation. This, I thought to myself, is the essence of life. This is what it all narrows down to when everything else is stripped away. And what was that tiny strand, which was all that was left when the sensations and emotions had all been purged through my brain? It was love, or God, or compassion. That night, I called it love. But I soon realized, as I tried to explain my experience to friends, that that word means something different to everyone, and is therefore useless as a description of my experience. It was pureness of heart, a fine, bright flame of compassion, a thread of pure gold that was left after my transfiguring experience. And this, I thought to myself, is what I must learn to take with me from this experience into the rest of my life. This is the purpose of my life, and the only thing that can give it meaning.

That night, my experience concluded when Susan, the night nurse, came on duty at midnight (three hours after this whole episode had begun). I told her I had seen the face of God, and that it was the face of my friend Edel. She smiled and held my hand for a bit and then went to get me a sleeping pill. I think she understood the power of my experience, but of course there was no way she could know its contents or its consequences for the rest of my life.

And this is what I am still exploring now, six months later. Edel has left San Francisco for a new life in Taos with his new lover, Aldous. Edel could not stand the intensity of my experience, and could not take responsibility for my continuing growth. I have sought out a psychic healer, a meditation teacher, a homeopathic practitioner, an acupuncturist, and various kinds of body-workers as I sort through the experience of that night. I'm not sure I understand what happened to me, except that it launched me on a quest for meaning in the rest of my life. As Dante says, midway through the journey of life, I found myself lost in the woods. In a sense, I saw hell and purgatory that night, and even caught a glimpse of paradise. Bringing all of this into my life and work is a continuing challenge.

Since the experience I have described here, my life has changed completely. I have become a regular student in Buddhist meditation classes. I volunteer regularly in hospitals and hospices in my community. I have learned Reiki and Swedish/Esalen-massage, and I work as a volunteer with people who are in the process of approaching their own deaths. I feel as though my experience has given me a unique insight into the process of dying, as well as endowing me with an unusual ability to see the karmic threads that link people together, both the living and the dead. People who are on the threshold of death seem to me to have a unique ability to observe this interconnectedness, and those of us who were fortunate enough to have come back can use this knowledge to help everyone around us.

In addition, I plan to move my photographic studio and my life to Berlin, Germany, in 2002. This is a direct result of the vision I had that night of my German friend, Edel, and his role in my life. Since Edel is dying of AIDS, I feel as though I need to fulfill his destiny and carry out the mission that he has attempted to achieve: teaching the rest of the world to see and to respect this interconnectedness, and to spread joy and loving kindness wherever I can. And MY karma leads me to Berlin.

A Pilgrim
in an
Unholy Land

I was born in 1952 into a pioneer Nevada ranching family. I grew up in rural Nevada surrounded by beautiful deserts, mountains, and valleys, but very little contact with people outside of my immediate family. Most of the people in my early life were those associated with ranching, relatives, the Catholic church and my father's few friends who all shared a common love for Italian opera, especially Puccini. This was the fertile soil in which the seed of myself was planted.

I remember the three greatest influences in my early life were the Catholic church, the natural and healthy surroundings of living in the country, and music, especially opera. I always had a strong sense of being different from my classmates, the few playmates I had, and my family. Because I was so drawn to the Catholic church and to music, it seemed logical as a child to seek to become a priest and a musician, something which the Catholic church encourages. This did not sit well with my parents, for whom the church was nothing more than a duty of the family. But the sense of being different persisted, and I always interpreted this difference to mean that I had a vocation to the priesthood.

I was an odd child—very religious, always serious, tall, thin, and anti-anything that did not fit tightly into my little fantasy world of religion and music. I am also dyslexic, a fact I did not discover about myself until I was in my middle thirties, which undoubtedly has influenced my perceptions. But for all my oddness, I have never been complacent, for I have always been on an endless quest for something, forever within my reach, but always just out of grasp.

When I was seventeen, being a loner, very tall (6'8.75") and a high school sophomore, the pressure to conform to the "accepted" role of a male teenager was too great. Giving in to the pressure of my peers and teachers, I joined the basketball team mid-season. Within two weeks I became very ill and one night, very early in the pre-dawn hours, I was rushed by my father to the nearest hospital twenty miles away in the nearest large town. By early morning I was on the operating table being operated on for acute appendicitis.

I died during that operation and was later revived. How long I was dead, I do not know. Later, I was told that the appendix ruptured as it was being removed. I was placed into intensive care for three days, although I was never told that I had died and was revived. My mother told me that I awoke once within this three-day period.

Very calmly I responded to her question of, "How are you?" by saying, "I am an exile from Greece." Whatever this means, I do have a sense that it is connected to the near-death experience.

I always wondered what really happened that morning. Getting information out of my parents—information that they thought was essential for their children to know—was totally impossible (though perhaps they had no idea how to explain any of this to me). I do know that after that experience, everyone treated me differently and gazed upon me in wonder and disbelief. My father encouraged me from this time onward to become a doctor. In a sense, I have pursued his wish, though not as a medical doctor but as a doctor of sacred science.

The sense of being different increased within me.

Though I had an inkling of being a gay man at seventeen, the difference I felt I still interpreted to my having a strong vocation for the priesthood. I had no clue that this difference might be my emerging feelings of being a gay man.

Of course, once I consciously realized I was a gay man, much of the differentness seemed to fade away. But, some of the differentness persisted, and this differentness I interpret to be my own near-death experience. This experience has left me with the feelings that *I am a pilgrim in an unholy land.* That is, this is an exclusive patriarchal society we live in that seeks to keep the status quo intact. It is this urge to understand my differentness that has fueled my life-long quest. I am attempting to identify this differentness and what it means, and to learn from my experience what will have value to others. Since mystical Christianity seemed to open the way for my quest, I logically began my quest seeking to understand this mystical tradition.

Actually, all my life I have been drawn to the mystical dimension of Christianity, though brought up in the Catholic tradition that still teaches it is the only authentic Christian tradition. As a child, I was totally convinced that this was so. This mystical longing increased after the above mentioned hospital experience, but I had to undergo my quest alone. No one, especially not my parents, was going to assist me in my quest (no one I had met had been through a near-death experience, and I believe the experience could not be shared in language that non-participants would understand).

My parents' response to everything is to ignore all questions and outside influences, especially the church, and then conform to the tradition of the family. I have often wondered if my attraction to the church is the result of rebelling against this strong family center I was raised within: Dad is God; Mom is God's Divine Consort. The male children are taught to become exact clones of God the Father (Dad) and the female children are to become clones of the Blessed Mother (Mom), the Divine Consort of God. If the children do not become clones on their own, then they must be forced into becoming clones or suffer the consequences. This is the family religion I was taught to submit to and obey without question. So I rebelled and went my own way, searching for my family—the opposite of my birth family.

So searching alone through the mystical Christian tradition, I was drawn strongly into its illuminating teaching. The deep dark secrets of the mystical tradition became alive within me. At least for my part, they all made sense and I understand them all clearly. This is very threatening knowledge for a young adult to be given. My family considers me crazy for seeking endlessly the knowledge that gives me meaning to my life. Instead, I should be working hard every day at a job I hate and make lots of money so I can buy more things I do not need. Then one day, I can retire so *then* I can begin to live life.

My church family considered me to be a heretic, for my interpretation of the church's teaching which differs from the official party line. And yet all the scripture and the writings of saints that I read and studied, I could see myself within, clearly and distinctly.

Not consciously knowing I had died and then been revived was the veil that was keeping my quest ever in the dark. If I had known I had died, been told by my doctor or parents, perhaps a lot of pain and feelings of hopelessness could have been avoided. But, even though I still have not been told by my parents of this experience, I know without a doubt that it did take place. The experience returns to me in times of great weakness and stress, and in my dreams at night. Twice more I was to be hospitalized for severe illnesses, and each time I either had another near-death experience, or I returned to the first one so I could relearn what the first experience's purpose was. Each time I recovered to full health. Yet I was lonelier and more determined to continue my quest no matter how costly— materially or emotionally.

I know deeply within that illness is not the result of germs and viruses—the modern demons and evil spirits—but the soul deeply troubled when a person is forced to fit into a clearly defined social hierarchy that ignores the person's place within the cosmic hierarchy. Illness is the result of listening to one's peers, parents, and religious authorities and not hearing one's own heart and following what the heart directs.

So, by my late teens, I left the Catholic church looking for an interpreter or religion to teach me and help me in my understanding of the vision, if you will, that I feel and continue to experience. I became a member of the late Jesus People movement, for even then the Jesus People movement was dying in California and was seeking new growth in rural Nevada. I was accepted for who I was, except when the new church discovered I was raised a Catholic—the most heinous crime imaginable.

Because I seemed to belong, I repressed my Catholic upbringing and became a Protestant. I stayed with the Jesus People for a few years, but was increasingly being delusioned in their exclusive mission of conquest without having any compassion for the contents of other religions. I never understood the deep hate these "Christians" felt for Christians of another faith (and I still do not understand). So I left the Jesus People, seeking something that would sustain me without seeking to destroy me.

After completing a year and a half of music studies at the University of Nevada, Reno, I moved out of the element I grew up in and finished my music studies at the California State University in Sacramento. It was here that I came to understand myself as a gay man and also a Christian too through the help of the then just budding Metropolitan Community Church. But in the early days of MCC I experienced the same hatred for anything Catholic by these so-called ecumenical Christians, so I returned to the more traditional churches and still kept my link with MCC alive. The traditional church fed my spiritual yearnings and MCC fed my gay yearnings—an unbalanced compromise. Living in California offered me numerous resources to further my independent study of religious thought and interpretation.

The open California culture I was in now was so vastly different from the closed Nevada culture I grew up in that it seemed I had left the country and gone to a different planet. The strong feelings I felt for my still unknown near-death experience (having no conscious information from any outside source to draw upon to tell me that this was a real experience), were reinforced by the new environment, adding fuel to my quest for inner truth. I dreamed nightly about the near-death experience, having dreams with great musical scores surpassing my favorite composers of this period of my life (such as Shostakovich, Tchaikovsky, and Rachmaninoff). It didn't take long to conclude that what I was feeling inside was deeply connected to the music of the Russian masters. And, being a student of history, I understood that the art of an artist reflects the culture the artist lives in. So I began my study of Russian culture and religion.

After years of study, I found that the Russian Orthodox Church preserved the many near-death experiences of its members throughout the centuries. This issue is not discussed openly anywhere in the literature or rites of this church, but to me it is expressed clearly in its temples, rituals, writings, and music, if one has the eye and ear of his heart open. Once I made the connection, a system of thought was already in place, handed down to this generation by a long tradition. This traditional language helps to explain what I experienced, though I had to adapt the traditional language into a language of my own. Understanding of my near-death experience is becoming clearer and clearer each day as I continue to connect and interpret my experience with respect to traditional experiences collected in what is now the Russian Orthodox Church. Much of how I understand the Orthodox Church is in my own explanation of my near-death experience. Much of the symbolism draws heavily on the iconography used in the liturgies of Ancient Egypt adapted by the Orthodox Church in Alexandria in the third, fourth, and fifth centuries of the Common Era. This symbolism became the mystical foundation for all the Christian Orthodox Churches.

So here, after finding a language in which I can express my thoughts, is my experience in 1969 as I recall it now:

I'm in a very dark place. I am totally aware of myself and yet I can see nothing, neither foot nor hand nor any part of my body. And yet I am keenly aware of all that is about me and can even see myself from a witness view without seeing any physical characteristic. This darkness is all about me. There is no place to run. I am aware of all, but I do not have any physical movements, no energy to move, whether motor activity or animation. I am frozen in place. I look before me, and even though I cannot move my head or eyes, my eyes of their own accord, beyond all rational thought, move to a point that is ahead of me on a gently yet increasingly rising incline. At the furthest distance, I see a pin point of white-yellow light. I must move to this light. I seem to float towards this without bodily movement. I slowly climb higher and higher towards this light. I must reach this light before it is too late—too late for what? I do not know, but I know that it is too late for something, just outside of memory and yet just before me. I cannot recall what it is that is nagging me, and yet it is there. I am not worried. Actually, I am not afraid of anything, not even of the darkness about me. A new thought—I have always been terrified of the dark, always seeing creatures grabbing at me, reaching out to do bodily harm to me in the dark. I see none of them now. I am at peace, floating towards a light that is more essential to me than anything else that I reach out for. I am alone. No one else is with me, but that is not new, for even though I have parents and siblings, I have always felt alone and lonely. It is as if I am walking in a desert alone, even though there is sand beneath my feet and a bush here and there, an animal or reptile or any other creature with me, I am still alone. Not that my immediate family are strangers or creatures, they are just different and I am not like them. I am an ancient soul in a new body. I am an ancient soul on a forever journey towards the light in a new body, able to acknowledge those about me and recognize them as new or old souls. How I can do this I do not know. I seek to be near those who are old souls like me, whom I feel comfortable around without having to justify my existence to them. The people I seek to be around and to love are old souls, just like me. I am alone now. In the darkness I am alone and yet aware of the old souls about me. I am loved for who I am in the darkness, but I want to be more than loved. I want to love and be loved; to feel and be felt without justification. I am in the darkness alone but not afraid. I am dancing towards the light without moving. I am a body without a body: I feel and love and yet do not have physical substance. I am essence. I am being. I Is. I's Is. Is-Is. Isis. I am. Light is moving closer or am I dancing forward. I cannot tell. The darkness fades, the light increases. Suddenly all I see before me is light and though I can see behind me without knowing how, all I see is darkness. I see, as a witness, my face, my left hand and right foot up to just a few inches from the knee, in the light. I can see each feature clearly except for those still in the darkness. I see nothing, no back of head, shoulders, back, left foot, right hand, etc...in the darkness. I, as I am, am looking now at the unknowable source of the light. Now I see, as a witness, myself rejoined to myself in joyous rapture, caught in mid-air after having jumped up with a great radiant expression on my face with my left hand clenched and my arm pulled down before me with my knees bent and a great sound emitting from my lips "Yes!" Now I see all of my body even though I, as the witness, am facing myself in the gate, and as this rapture of myself before me. Myself, as a witness, has no body, voice, or locomotion—only awareness. The I am that is in the gate is now, as the witness, whom I turn all my attention towards. My rapture of myself is yet to be... At the source is a ball of golden light emitting beams of rainbows that float like ribbons through the golden-white light towards me. All the souls who have ever made this journey, through the gate where I am now, are there in the ball of gold. Each soul is emitting its essence as a color in each of the joint ribbons with other souls. Each soul has a color of the seven colors of the rainbow. My own color is blue or red—I can't clearly distinguish. Each ribbon is the co-joining of seven souls. It is the blue/red color that my own soul is seeking to join. I recognize that all souls are equal, but each soul has its own distinct color. The ribbons of rainbows are all floating about in a harmony that generates sound. Each soul has its own pitch and vibration. Each ribbon has its own melody. Now I hear a chorus of voices, then the orchestra of instruments, then an orchestra with voices, then a small family of one type of instrument, then a solo, a quartet, a duo, a trio, until all combinations have sounded. And then silence, which is the clearest and most joyous of all. The golden ball emits all this and more—thoughts, feelings, ideas, every vibration infinitely possible. The golden ball, the face of the unknowable source, stretches infinitely in all directions. I continue to dance forward, but something within tells me to go no further. I am trapped, not negatively but positively, in the gate. I cannot go forward nor backward until I do something. What? What? Love. Love. Love another old soul I know and see in my dreams, but cannot name. My other self, my other half, if you will. I see and I think I have found. But the soul I feel so comfortable about and seek, does not recognize me. What to do? Is this really my other half? Am I just seeking any old soul to join, commune, or become one with? This other old soul is either blue or red, or I am either blue or red—I cannot tell. But we must join together, the blue/red. I do not know with certainty. I must continue to seek. I am uncertain. I am at a loss. All my questions stem from this point. No one can give me that answer except the other old soul itself—and then not with words, but with silence that is felt and heard. The other old soul will certainly recognize me when we meet. I know this for certain. I know this is truth, the realization I have been seeking. Every old and new soul my heart yearns for, I look at their faces: Is this my partner? Is this my love? Is this my healer? I now know I cannot go beyond the point in the gate where I am; I can't enter any further into the holiest of holies until what I have done in eons past has been healed. I must heal this old soul I seek and this other old soul will heal me. We both did violence to each other and we both must heal this violence into love. We are both stuck in different gates seeking to dance forward, but cannot until we are joined together. Even if this current body dies, I cannot dance any further until I actively seek to heal what I have made ill. My soul will return again if I do not, and all this will be repeated. I now know what must be done. My fear and uncertainty have been faced and what was unknown in my unconscious is now conscious. And yet I have always known this, but would not confront it face to face. I have been avoiding this moment for over 30 years. This other old soul is my right hand and left foot—the rest of my body that is still in the darkness. My body that is in darkness is now reaching the light of day.

The dawning is near…the joining is at hand! The bells are beginning to sound!

This is the vision of my near-death experience. You will notice that I am not greeted by personages in the darkness before I enter the gate. I believe that since I was born and raised in isolation and at seventeen, none of the people who were close to me had yet died, there was no one to meet with me on the other side and guide me. As a Catholic, the person of Jesus is never stressed and you are never taught that you will see Jesus after you die. So this teaching was not in my memory when this experience occurred. As Catholics, we are taught that there are angels and saints with us at all times. In a sense, even though I did not see the saints' nor angels' faces, I did have a sense of their presence with me.

The vision of the unknowable source, which others might call God (which to me is a very narrow term for a very immense perception), is, of course, the center of the vision.

If one is familiar with the Divine Liturgy used in any of the Orthodox churches, you will recognize the gate in the iconostasis, and especially the light of the liturgy served in the early hours of Pascha. Much of my own vision is plainly seen in the Orthodox liturgies. Some comes from my study of ancient pre-Christian liturgies—Jewish, Egyptian, Greek, Roman, and Sumerian. Whether I have borrowed from these and formulated my own mythology, I do not know. But I do know I see connections with my remembrance of the experience and what has been traditionally sent down to us from the past/present.

As a gay man, I am still hopeful about finding my life companion who will support, teach, heal, and perhaps guide me. This is the only piece of the mosaic I have yet to have a direct experience of. Every other element in the vision I have had direct experience of in my daily life except for the life companion whom I must find to heal and who will heal me, in order to complete the cycle of the vision. If this does not happen, I will have to go through the vision again. If I survive the next close encounter—the next journey to the gate— perhaps I will find my companion. If I remember what I now consciously understand, perhaps that was all I was supposed to discover and I will pass through the gate never to return.

If I have learned nothing else from my own experience and the ancient experiences of tradition, it is this—the purpose of the tradition is to teach each individual how to die without being killed or committing suicide. If any individual takes his own life or allows others to do it for him, then they will return and repeat the whole process again. If any individual seeks to live life fully and then dies *not through their own design*, they will not return to repeat the whole process.

The quest for meaning of the vision is concluded. What comes next in my journey, I have no idea. But at least my own near-death experience is clearer than it was yesterday or the day before yesterday.

1. Did sexual identity come into play during your NDE?

None whatsoever.

2. After the NDE, did the near-death experience change your sexual identify in any way or change the way you feel about your sexual identity?

It made me reach the realization that all conditioned social pressures were (and are) control issues and no matter what I do or who I am, including sexuality, makes no difference one way or the other. That is, all the social commandments and rules are structured to give a few power over the majority of people, but these regulations have no value or worth in the next plane of existence. Only holding everything as sacred and holy determines one's passage in this life into the next. If sex is mutual and loving between two adults of the same gender, it does not matter an iota. But if sex is rape, giving one person power over another, this is not sacred and it will make the passage in this life difficult and make the next plane a living hell and not a paradise. All is sacred and essential to well-being and abundant life, past, present, and future.

A PRAYER WARRIOR

Presently I am in my 50s and am on disability. I live in New York City in a small village type apartment on the east side of Manhattan on a fifth floor walk-up with the tub in the kitchen and under the roof. Being disabled, this is not an easy task and one has to keep a sense of humor at all times. My work consists of witnessing and giving my testimony about Jesus Christ and all that he has done for me.

I guess what I am still learning, with a great deal of difficulty, is not to take on the pain of others, no matter who they are. I can feel compassion and try to help, but must strive not to be led by my emotions and feelings, which get me into major trouble. Since no one in my family ever communicated with each other, I witnessed my sister Lucille's suffering and took on her pain, which re-directed my entire life and threw me into major depression and terror. She was the oldest and the most beautiful and brilliant of us all—there were five girls in all. The youngest, Diane, was from another man, not from my father. My parents were divorced when I was about four-years old and we all went into an orphanage and then my mother got us back and took us back home! To make a very long story short, my sister Lucille's journey was a very brutal one. In 1979, she froze to death in a condemned building in Coney Island where she laid on the floor for three months until someone found her (or what was left of her). I found out about it on the six o'clock news. You can imagine my horror! There are really no words to express how I felt. There are questions that will never be answered as to what really happened to her. Did she remember me, since we hadn't spoken for many years after losing touch with one another? My sister Sandy, who was in contact with her towards the end of her life, never picked up the phone and expressed concern that Lucille needed help. She also was a barrier between Lucille and her children. Lucille's daughter, Mercy (she had three girls and a boy living in Alabama) was trying to reach her and take her back home where she could have been taken care of (and would still be alive today). My sister Sandy wouldn't give me their addresses .

It took me so many years to find out where they were and to obtain their phone numbers. Sandy waited a year and half before she contacted Lucille's children and told them that Lucille died of natural causes. Since then she refuses to speak about this horrific situation. She has screamed and hollered at me for going to Alabama to meet with the children. She doesn't want anyone talking to each other because somewhere deep down inside there is guilt that she will not admit to.

We are all guilty of neglect. As you can see, my family is very dysfunctional. There are tremendous amounts of pain and scars from the past that have to heal. I am still trying to heal from the trauma. I took on my sister Lucille's pain, which shaped and almost destroyed my life. This is one of the reasons I wound up clinically dead in 1974 or thereabouts. The hospital told me my records are gone now. I don't have actual dates or anything recorded about my NDE experience of clinical death. The NDE occurred at at Bellevue Hospital, of all places—like that terrible movie *Snakepit*!

The other thing I am now learning on a daily basis is to love myself and hold myself with tenderness and know that I am truly a child of God. I am loved and deserve to have a life of quality, to laugh, to sing and to dance. My life is as important as anyone else's. I am also learning with a great deal of difficulty not to give my power away to anyone else and, after so many years, listen to my own intuition.

During the 1960's, I had an experience where the Virgin Mary came to me—twice—once at work where the whole office disappeared and once walking near 2nd Avenue and 14th Street. I lived on 2nd Avenue and 18th Street at that time. She never spoke to me, but she was shimmering in incredible colors and had a very soft and loving expression on her face. Everything—all my surroundings—disappeared when this happened. The Blessed Mother was surrounded by awesome colored light and peace and love was everywhere. It just about took my breath away!

My next experience was with Marilyn Monroe a year after my near-death experience—around 1975. I was on the 1st Avenue bus going home with 400 downs (pills of every color, shape, and size) in a shopping bag to over-dose again. I spoke to no one about what I was going to do. By accident I jumped up to get off the bus at my old stop on 18th street where I lived in the 1960s. In my head, I never moved out of that period of time and that apartment I loved in the 1960s. As I was getting off the bus, I saw a black and yellow bus stop sign outside the door. I realized I was getting off at the wrong stop as I didn't live there any more. I said to myself "J.C. what are you doing? You don't live here anymore." I got back on the bus all shook up as I had never done this before. I sat down in another seat and next to me was a piece of paper. I picked it up and turned it over. It was the cover of a book someone had been reading which said Norma Jean Baker. There was a picture of Marilyn Monroe on the cover. I put the paperback down and as I looked up, Marilyn Monroe was boarding the bus. She had on a long terry cloth bathrobe, deep purple, and messed-up blonde curls. She died in 1962, the year when I graduated from high school. This was 1975. She walked up to me, we looked at each other, and she sat down next to me on my left. I knew no one else could see her but me. When I got up to get off the bus at 25th street, she followed me. We walked down the street together and up the five flights. We did not speak in public. She sat in one chair and I sat in another. She looked sad and said to me, "If you do this, you will regret it for eternity." She said God sent her to me and she also said she wanted to come back, but she couldn't. She also said that she did not kill herself. Again, she repeated, "If you do this, you will regret it for eternity." Just like she came to me, she got up and left right, *through* the door. I started shaking all over and got down on my knees by the tub in the kitchen and sobbed. God spoke to me and said, "When I call for you, that's when you come to me." I got up and flushed the 400 pills down the toilet.

I am here now to speak about it. It is like getting hit with a bolt of lightening when something like this happens. I kept everything in all these years, because the few people I told said, "You're nuts!" So I stopped speaking for many years— until 1990 when God came to me when I was ill and told me, "Speak out." I have been speaking out since then and here I am today.

Before my NDE, I was very depressed and ill from 13 shock treatments which backfired. Everything I wanted to forget I remembered bigger than life and everyday things like my address and phone numbers were all forgotten. I didn't even recognize New York City when I was released from the hospital, two blocks from my house. I lived with my boyfriend for 20 years (before and after the NDE) and it was not a good relationship. There was a lot of anguish. I was disabled with rheumatoid arthritis and, in 1990, I had a physical crisis. I was crippled in bed for six months. Then I started a detox and changed my diet with the help of my boyfriend's mother.

After detoxing and changing my diet and being so grateful to walk again and so overwhelmed that God gave me another chance, I went back to my roots. I became born again into the family of Jesus and God, like I was when I was five years old in Williamsburg, Brooklyn. As soon as I could walk, I went to Times Square Church and got baptized. I am a Messianic Jew and a believer in Jesus Christ, Amen.

While I was on my path and my boyfriend was on his, we got farther and farther apart. He became violent and attacked me physically. I wound up in a women's shelter in Brooklyn, completely traumatized. Finally after a lot of prayer, I found my lease and went to the 13th precinct in my neighborhood. I showed them my lease and told them if I didn't get my apartment back, someone would die. Four policemen escorted me to the apartment and handcuffed my boyfriend; they took him to jail. Later, I dropped the charges. Since then, we have been friends. He is bed-bound and lives around the corner from me. I shop and clean and run errands for him.

Since then, I met Robert and am very happy with him. He lives in Westchester and we go back and forth between his house and mine. In Westchester—New Rochelle—I listen to the birds and whistle and talk to them all the time. After feeding them sunflower seeds, sunflowers came up in the garden. Now I take care of the lawn out there, gardening for the first time in my life. This is truly a dream come true to be in the country. Robert says, "This is not the country. It's too civilized."

I love the trees and birds. What a kiss from God to grow my own sunflowers for the first time!

And so this is my job: to spread love, peace and joy with Jesus Christ, the Living God. This is my job and again, I am so very grateful to tell people about Jesus, and that I can't wait to join him. Thank you so much for helping me tell my story, to spread the good news to anyone who will listen. God Bless you.

1. Did sexual identity come into play during your NDE?

No, not at all.

2. After the NDE, did the near-death experience change your sexual identify in any way or change the way you feel about your sexual identity?

No, not until recently (1990s). After reading the Bible, I feel I would like to be in a heterosexual relationship— at this time anyway.

I WAS SWIMMING IN AN OCEAN OF ECSTASY

First Near-Death Experience

My first near-death experience was in September of 1985. The accident occurred on a Friday around six in the evening, as I was riding my bicycle home from work in San Francisco. I was working for a temp agency at the time, on a long-term assignment in a downtown office. I had taken to riding my bike back and forth, as it was so fast and convenient.

I remember thinking what a beautiful day it was, typical Indian Summer weather for that time of year. Ironically, it was the one day I was running late and I had forgotten my bike helmet. As a result, I was riding with extra caution, and attempting to stay clear of heavy traffic.

I was crossing Market Street at a fairly rapid speed, when my front tire slipped through a crack in the metal grating which is a part of the BART (subway train) ventilation system. Apparently, a cross piece of metal was missing or broken off and created just enough space for a bike tire to slip through. The impact was so sudden, it was like hitting a brick wall. The force of the impact sent me crashing head-first onto the metal grating. My face hit the jagged perforation designed to help keep tires from skidding in wet weather.

Immediately after the impact from falling forward onto the metal grating, I felt myself floating up, out of my body. I was hovering above my body. All the people who were watching it seemed paralyzed by shock and horror at what had happened. I think they assumed that I was dead.

I remember looking down and seeing my body three-dimensionally for the first time. It was such a shock, because we usually never see ourselves except in a one-dimensional mirror reflection, or a photograph. But I felt no pain at all. I felt completely whole and free, and I thought, "This is who I really am." I saw my physical body, all crumpled and bloody and lifeless. This enormous wave of compassion washed over me and I wanted to tell all of the bystanders that everything was going to be OK and not to be sad or alarmed.

Then suddenly I felt myself being pulled, literally at the speed of light, farther from the physical earth. I saw all of the people on the planet simultaneously in that one moment. I saw people in China and Sweden and Uruguay. I saw people sleeping and dreaming. I saw people preparing food in their homes and in restaurants, people traveling in all manner of transportation to and from work, school and appointments. I saw children playing together and bankers and teachers and factory workers at their jobs. I saw mothers giving birth to children, which was especially beautiful and moving to me.

I saw people in hospitals and prisons, mental institutions and nursing homes and orphanages who felt desperately alone, abandoned and afraid. And I saw people painting pictures, planting gardens, writing stories, composing music and people dancing.

I saw people praying in mosques and temples, synagogues, and churches—people individually expressing their own silent prayers. I saw indigenous tribes in all different parts of the world drumming and chanting. And God was sending multitudes of angels to the earth, to assist in answering all of the countless millions of prayers being offered up at that single moment.

As I seemed to move further into the light, I saw the earth as though from outer space. It was like a beautiful, shimmering blue and green jewel floating in the cosmos. As I moved closer, I saw that the earth was vibrating and pulsating, as though it was a living, breathing entity and not just some physical mass. And I thought, "This is Mother Earth; this is our Divine Mother." But as I looked even closer, I saw that there were terrible wounds and sores on different parts of her body. She was gasping for breath, and calling out to God and to her children to stop the killing and destruction and hatefulness. She was dying and praying for all of us to help her to heal and regenerate. Again I felt overwhelmed by feelings of sadness and compassion. I desired to hold Mother Earth in my arms—to whisper words of love and hope.

I remember that a part of me felt frustrated and powerless to actually do anything of value—just as I have often felt in my physical body. Yet another part of me felt completely powerful, as though there was nothing that I couldn't accomplish. At that moment I asked God, "What do you want me to do?" And the answer that came to me was that I had to go back into my physical body in order to complete certain goals that had already been set into motion. And I thought, "But I can't go back because my body is too far gone; it's beyond repair." And I was also afraid that I could never accomplish (with all of my physical limitations) all that I could do as a spirit form, which felt so free and unencumbered.

I remember feeling angry and fearful about going back, after being in all of this light—to have to go back to the darkness. And then I felt the presence of Jesus Christ all around me. The feeling of love was completely overwhelming. I felt as though I was swimming in an ocean of ecstasy. And I asked Him, "Do I really have to go back?" And His answer was that I was a part of God's divine plan, as is every person, and that my ultimate purpose is to love and serve God and all sentient beings. And I could tell that He understood all of my fear and doubt. He assured me that I would heal and recover, but that it would be a lifelong process. I did have the power within me, though I hadn't realized it until now that all I had to do was to ask for the courage and strength to persevere in my life and in my work. This particular information held enormous value for me. I had often questioned whether I would ever really find a place in the world—having always been somewhat of an outsider— a place where my passionate concern regarding so many compelling modern issues could somehow take solid form. I wanted to make even a small difference.

Then Christ said that He would send me guardian angels to aid me in my healing, and guide and protect me. Then the light became even brighter, and suddenly there were angels everywhere, playing the most transcendentally beautiful music, and singing "Hosanna!" and hymns of praise to God. And some of the angels were crying—which I didn't understand. And Jesus said that the angels were weeping tears of joy for my new life on earth and that they were also expressing compassion for the hardship I would endure for the rest of my earthly existence. And He said that He had summoned the angels to guide me on my journey back to the earth and to my physical body. I remember feeling so grateful that Christ was there to help me to understand everything that was happening. I also remember feeling that I wasn't afraid anymore. No one could ever hurt me again—I would try my best every day to do God's will.

I awakened to find two men kneeling over me with expressions of apprehension and concern on their faces. For some reason I felt they might be gay men. They both looked to be in their thirties. I couldn't help but notice how handsome they both were. They were beautifully dressed in what appeared to be very expensive business clothes. I remember thinking that they might be some kind of executives working for a corporation, which in fact is exactly what they turned out to be. One of the men obviously had some type of first aid training, and had monitored my vital signs. They informed me that an ambulance was on its way and to try to remain still and not speak. That was easy to do, considering the extent of my injuries. They had both taken off their jackets and lain them over me. I was horrified to discover that the jackets were covered with blood and completely ruined. I remember feeling embarrassed and yet, I felt enormously grateful for the kindness of these two strangers. Their presences were completely warm and comfortingand made me feel safe and protected.

They waited alongside me until the ambulance came, and then came to the hospital to make sure I was properly attended to. They visited me in the hospital on two separate occasions. I made a somewhat feeble offer to replace their ruined clothes, but they simply laughed it off, and insisted that the only thing that mattered was that I was alive and more or less in one piece. Again, their presence filled me with a sense of hope and courage. I felt very strongly that both men symbolized what would prove to be a succession of "angels" that Christ had promised to send me. In fact, this turned out to be truer than I could possibly have imagined.

Second Near-Death Experience

The summer that Richard died was 1990. I was apartment-sitting for my friend Ellen, who was vacationing in Hawaii. I was beginning to feel that I had pretty much worn out my welcome in Marin County, which is just north of San Francisco. I was still having terrible physical and emotional problems stemming from the bicycle accident. Also, being a gay man in a largely bedroom community like Marin County is the ultimate frustration. I had never felt more like a stranger in a strange land. I was deeply depressed and drinking excessive amounts of alcohol. On top of that, I had met someone that I felt extremely attracted to while knowing nothing good would come of it—story of my life!

I seemed destined to drift forever, from one job and living situation to another; never really having any money (or a life) to speak of. I even started to make a mental list of all the different jobs I had held, beginning to think that I probably qualified for the Guinness Book of World Records. I felt as though I had struggled and worked harder than anyone on the face of the planet! I had virtually nothing to show for it. I also felt more estranged from family and friends than ever before. It was as though my life consisted of an endless series of failures and humiliations and unnamed fears. Looking back now, I can see that it was really a fear of success that caused me to sabotage myself.

I had been thinking a lot about my friends, Joseph and Richard. I hadn't seen either of them for quite a long time, and they were suddenly very much on my mind. I made a mental note to call them that night. Later that day, as I was walking home, the strangest thing happened.

Directly on the other side of a cyclone fence that separated the bungalow apartments from a large open grassy field, a fawn was sitting on its haunches, perfectly still and staring at me. I very slowly moved closer to the animal and crouched down directly in front of it. I naturally thought that the doe had to be injured, not to react to my close proximity and run away. I said something very softly—don't remember what—and as I looked into the fawn's eyes, this inexplicable and overwhelming feeling of sadness came to me. I went into the apartment to call the Marin SPCA to report the fawn.

Later that evening, I remembered to call Richard and Joseph. Joseph answered the phone, and the moment I identified myself, I sensed that something was wrong. There was a long pause, and then Joseph informed me that Richard had died. I couldn't believe I had heard him right and I was speechless as I struggled to think of something to say. I think I finally said something like, "That's impossible."

As Joseph explained the almost incomprehensible circumstances surrounding Richard's death, I could hardly believe what I was hearing. There was an element of complete unreality about all of it. Eventually, Joseph gave me the time and date of the memorial service, and I promised to be there.

Two days later, I drove Ellen's truck into the city to attend Richard's service. As Richard and I didn't move in the same circles, I knew very few people at the service. I sat far back in the church alone. The service was, at least for me, both sorrowful and joyful at the same time. Joseph indicated to me later that this was what Richard wanted. The service certainly reflected Richard's love of music and dance, and all of his life-affirming qualities that made him such a warm and loving person. To everyone who knew him, he was a very special person. It wasn't until much later that I learned from Joseph that, while in the hospital, Richard came out of his coma long enough to tell Joseph that it was time for him to die in order to move on to another level. He told Joseph not to feel sad. (Richard had also dictated his own memorial service, the details of which Joseph carefully recorded.)

Later that evening, after I had returned to Ellen's bungalow, I sat all alone in silence in the kitchen, trying to make some sense of it all, but despite my best efforts, Richard's death remained impossibly premature and tragic. Also, we were so close in age and while Richard had everything to live for, I seemed to be living this nightmare existence. The same question kept coming back to me, over and over again: "Why him and not me?"

I couldn't remember when I'd had a decent night's sleep—insomnia was one of the many problems that had begun to afflict me since the accident. I still had some very strong sleeping pills which the doctor had prescribed a long time ago and which I had taken only once. I decided to take several to knock me out so that I could finally get some sleep. Then I remembered a large bottle of Cuervo Gold tequila that we had planned to make margaritas with (for Ellen's bon voyage party which never materialized). Although straight tequila is not my drink of choice, it was all there was. I sat in Ellen's kitchen with a large glass tumbler of tequila in front of me, letting my thoughts run free. A sense of frustration and futility had been creeping over me for a long period of time, exacerbated by Richard's death. I longed for nothing as much as a return to the light which I remembered from so long ago. I still don't believe that I actually harbored a desire to kill myself. It was more a desire to momentarily obliterate all thought and feeling, especially as I felt so powerless to really understand or control my destiny—if, indeed, I even had a destiny anymore.

I took several more sleeping pills and continued drinking the tequila. I kept waiting to feel tired, but instead, I felt strangely alert. Suddenly, I had an impulse to hear Ellen's *Red Octopus* album by the Grateful Dead. I thought this was

the ultimate irony as I had never cared for the Grateful
Dead. However, to be dead at that moment seemed a highly
desirable state for which I would feel more grateful. Perhaps
it was my desire to be reunited with Richard and to be back
"in the light," especially as my life seemed so unbearably dark
and pointless.

I took more pills and began gulping the tequila instead of
sipping it. As I sat there, I was suddenly overcome with the
thought that I was going to die at that moment, right there in
Ellen's kitchen in Fairfax, California. I thought I was going to
die this ignominious death as a failed artist, in a place I didn't
especially care to be. For a brief moment I felt a sense of
complete relief—that I was finally going to die and be
released from the pain and burden of trying to pursue my
dreams of becoming a filmmaker. I was obviously far too sick
and dysfunctional to accomplish much of anything. This
feeling was almost immediately followed by a sense of
personal betrayal. I saw myself failing everyone who had
supported and believed in me along the way (no matter how
estranged I felt from family and friends at the time). Worst of
all, I was betraying the information I had received from my
first near-death experience.

I was also betraying my lifelong struggle to express my
love for life and for people through my creativity which was,
after all, a gift from God. Suddenly I wanted to continue
living more than anything in the world, so that I could
continue to pursue my film project, even if it was against
seemingly insurmountable odds.

By that time the combination of ingesting an overdose of
sleeping pills, as well as copious amounts of alcohol, had
caused me to feel extremely muddled. My only thought was
to go next door and hope that my neighbor was home to take
me to the emergency room. I knew the situation was critical.

I started to move from the kitchen to the front door, in order to seek help. Halfway across the living room, I passed out.

All of a sudden I felt as though I was moving through a corridor. It was dark but not at all frightening. I sensed the presence of others. Some of these "spirit entities" were moving more slowly than others toward the light, as there seemed to be some unresolved fear and confusion and anxiety regarding a possible transition from the physical to the metaphysical world. Suddenly, I was in a place that appeared to be a room suffused with light. There were no walls or ceilings or floors. Light seemed to extend into infinity. Then, just as suddenly, I felt the presence of my friend Richard everywhere. He was inseparable from the light. My immediate thought was, "This is it. I'm finally dead, once and for all. I'm in heaven again, only this time I get to stay." Richard's spirit seemed all-pervasive and completely powerful, as though his emotional and intellectual capacities were incalculable. Our communication was telepathic and overlapping, so that the answers already existed before the questions could even be asked. It was as if our spirits were intertwined to the point that we were one and the same. Richard seemed to be smiling as he indicated that there were both good news and bad news. This was just as I remembered Richard. His extremely warm sense of humor had always shone through. He indicated that I was, in fact, only "visiting" (yet again), and that I would have to go back shortly. I thought to myself "Please, God. No! Not again!" Richard indicated that our time together would be brief, but that he had a great deal of information to reveal. He seemed to be able to address an unlimited number of thoughts and feelings simultaneously. He also seemed to have enormous empathy for the numerous problems related to my various physical and emotional states. He understood my seemingly endless struggles on so many levels, for such a protracted length of time. All of these struggles contributed to my sense of exhaustion and despair over my entire life up to that point.

Richard reviewed many far-reaching and intimate aspects of my life history that he had not known when he was in the physical world. He discussed the current zeitgeist as well as possible future events, always emphasizing the importance of free will within a Divine Plan. He elaborated on this point, seeming to regard history as being largely about people being in the right place at the right time. Richard also mentioned certain key people in my life over the years, explaining important and fascinating aspects of their own lives to me. He spoke of specific turning points in my life, especially my bicycle accident and the terrible aftermath. He also ruminated at length on the value of creating what he called a "personal mythology." He informed me that certain books and music would come into my life on this subject, which would inspire me on many levels. He also expounded on the healing process, which he insisted was essential for me to devote myself to. He indicated that I would be involved in co-producing a film which would, in part, help teach people how to heal themselves. This idea was remarkable to me, as the idea for our company's first feature film hadn't even occurred to me yet. Also, the theme of healing seemed so remote, as I am not a physician nor do I have a medical background.

Richard also talked about time as a "continuum," that I must learn how to experience and apply the fluid, non-linear qualities of time. Somehow, he knew of my great passion for the artist Michelangelo. Suddenly, to my amazement, I was transported to the time and place where Michelangelo was painting the Sistine Chapel. For a fleeting moment I actually *became* Michelangelo. The experience was staggering beyond words.

Richard then reflected on my childhood dream to one day become a filmmaker. He indicated that the screenplay I was constantly rewriting would eventually be made into a feature film and that it would achieve enormous artistic and financial success. He also gently admonished me for worrying all the time about everything—a trait I inherited from my father. Even though he went on at great length about my future film achievements, he also referred to me as a "doubting Thomas." Then an astonishing thing happened.

The space surrounding me seemed to go completely dark. The feeling was remarkably like that of being inside a movie theater, just as the lights are going down and the film is about to begin. I felt the same sense of excitement that I always do when this happens. And then I actually witnessed a scene from my screenplay, *This Life*, very much as I had written and visualized it. Only the scene was three-dimensional, like a hologram, so that I was both an observer as well as a silent, invisible participant. I was actually walking around inside of the scene, able to reach out and secretly touch the actors and other physical aspects of the set. The moment was so vibrant that even today I can still recount all of the colors and smells and sounds and textures. The whole scene was even more wonderful and compelling than I had imagined it could be.

Richard seemed acutely aware of my estrangement from my family and friends, as well as my self-loathing and self-destruction, which came largely from my negative feelings about my sexuality and sensitivity. He indicated most emphatically that I should openly celebrate and honor my sexuality as a precious gift from God. This was a startling revelation to me, especially after a lifetime of secrecy, fear and guilt.

I was also told that the angels operate from intuition, and that I must always remain aware and open to all of the "messages" occurring in my life, especially from this point on. I somehow knew this implied that I should encourage and appreciate time spent alone in order to be more sensitive and receptive to information being directed toward me. This information would ultimately serve to enrich and enhance my life on every level. I was filled with gratitude for this understanding.

Richard also discussed the Jungian concept of "meaningful coincidence" which I had first read about in Jean Shinoda Bolen's book, *The Tao of Psychology*. He elaborated on this in regards to the importance of people, places and situations. He seemed to imply that everything is imbued with great meaning and continually suggests new possibilities. He specifically pointed out the importance of women in my life, and that to tap into this feminine energy would continue to be extremely important for me. I have since dubbed my women friends the "Living Goddess Network." He also indicated that I would continue to meet both gay and non-gay men who, like myself, are seeking a more spiritual and compassionate way of being in the world.

Richard discussed AIDS as well as other illnesses and life-threatening diseases, mostly in metaphorical terms. He said that certain individuals leave their physical bodies at particular times in order to help facilitate critically important periods of rebirth and transformation on the earthly plane. Because I had always considered Richard a very spiritual person, his remarks helped me see his physical death in a very different way.

Richard indicated that it would soon be time for me to leave Marin County and return to my hometown of San Francisco, primarily to engage in certain events which would lead to the development of a unique creative endeavor. I felt a distinct sense of exhilaration at this news. Richard also forewarned me that things would become a lot worse before they became better. Given that things already seemed about as bad as it was possible for things to be, this was very alarming information to receive. He predicted a period of what he termed a "terrible darkness" out of which would come illumination. He told me that I was being sent back, not to suffer, but to ultimately create a work of art which would help to teach people the importance of self-love and acceptance. I would help teach people to believe in their own unique powers to heal themselves and the planet, as well as to express the boundless creativity and joy which resides within each person. Richard also promised to send me "guardian angels," a reiteration of the promise made to me during my first near-death experience.

I woke up feeling acutely sick to my stomach and spent what seemed like an eternity in the bathroom, vomiting. Since my neighbor was out, I called a taxi to take me to the nearest hospital. Even though I had eliminated the worst of the toxins, they still had to pump my stomach. Later, a very young-looking doctor came in. He exuded a warm and caring quality. He looked at me and said, "All things considered, it is amazing that you are still alive." At this, I burst into tears. As I began to calm down, the doctor asked me if I would like to speak to a therapist. I assured him that I was fine. After all, how could I begin to explain what had happened? I was afraid they would lock me up and throw away the key. Besides, all I wanted to do was get home as quickly as possible so that I could write down everything that Richard had communicated to me.

THE SECOND CHANCE

My name is Christopher. I work at a county hospital as an outpatient nurse in women's health care. I am 49 and have been in a relationship with my domestic partner who I love deeply for over 14 years. I am of mixed blood—Native American and Northern European. I have been sober for over 18 years and actively work a Spiritual Program to stay sober.

My near-death experience happened as the result of a deliberate overdose in 1973. When I tried to kill myself I was in deep despair and depression after having been raped and beaten and left for dead by a casual friend that a close male friend had referred to me as a roommate. I had been desperate for a place to live as I was homeless and very poor. My "friend" withheld the information that this man had beaten his prior roommate, a girlfriend, to the point of hospitalization for her injuries. After the rape, I felt numb, dazed. A week later I was mugged. The next place I moved to ended a few weeks later with a landlord move-in eviction. It was the last straw. I felt no desire to live, totally estranged from my life. I only wanted to end my pain. I absolutely did not believe in any Higher Power or seek any afterlife. I made seven overdose attempts in a 45 day period, bouncing in and out of psychiatric units for the city's poor. Being uneducated, I did not know which substance or how much to take. But practice almost makes perfect. With the last overdose I died.

I was brought by ambulance to a hospital emergency room. According to a witness who later told me about it, the staff of the ER worked on me as a Code Blue until the code was called off. Another emergency case came in and as the staff were leaving my bedside for that new case, I gasped and started breathing again. I do not know how long I was "dead" but days later when I came out of the coma my chest was still bruised from chest compressions made by the staff's attempts to revive me. My throat was raw from intubation. When I was aware of my surroundings, I said, "NO" and that's all I said for awhile.

My own memory of events during the emergency was very different. I felt a tremendous feeling of rushing, speeding of myself toward a brilliant warm white sparkly light, which did not hurt my eyes. This light was a warm shimmering one (since I had felt an icy cold despair inside, this was a huge difference). The tunnel I was hurtling through was composed of the hands of people who loved me. I could feel the hands and the presence of countless numbers of people whom I could not see except for their hands. These hands felt loving, and were holding me and nonjudgmentally guiding me. It was as if they were passing me through—not carrying me—just guiding me toward the light. I felt surrounded by the most intense peace that I had ever experienced. I felt myself inched toward this light and myself reaching towards it—complete acceptance and love. Then suddenly I stopped moving and I heard a voice deep inside my head say, "It's not time, you have to go back." (The voice was nether male nor female—I have tried to get clearer on this, but can only say it was neither sex.) I did not speak, but only said, "NOOOO" inside of my head. I knew I did not want to go back. Immediately afterwards I hurtled back in the other direction from which I had just come. The next thing I knew was that there were huge, harsh lights which hurt my eyes and I felt terrible pain. I was once again in the hospital psychiatric unit.

I did not tell anyone what I'd seen and heard. I was afraid my psychiatrist and others would think I was crazy, not just depressed, and would try to drug me. So I kept it a secret. I never made another suicide attempt and I did not tell my shrink why. I suddenly believed that I could have a life of less pain—that I did not have to die to have no pain. I knew that every day I breathed after the NDE I was choosing to live. I knew that death itself wasn't painful, though dying can be painful to the body. I realized there was something after death. I knew I was not supposed to choose my time of death. For the first time, I felt hope. I felt protected. These were all ideas I had never had before. However, I kept what had happened to me a secret, and I tried to forget.

Afterwards, I noticed an odd physical change which still persists. Every morning I cannot tolerate artificial light for several minutes when I first wake up. It is like I need time to adjust my eyes and then only with natural light. After awhile I can handle artificial light, but I never really like it. I did not have this sensitivity prior to my experience.

About three years after my experience I came out. I realized life was about risk and openness and honesty. I had been afraid for years of the label lesbian or gay. Because of my past, I came out only when I was sure I was going toward women and *not* away from men. I realized I had always been a lesbian.

Many years later, totally by accident, I found out about other people having near-death experiences. At the time, I was struggling to find some concept of a Higher Power to help me stay sober. I went to the movies for a triple bill, and thought a film I hadn't heard of before (called *Resurrection*) would be about gospel musicians. I started crying and hyperventilating when the actress in the movie had her near-death experience. All those years until the movie, I had kept my secret, afraid of what other people would think. I was staggered to find out others had had this experience. After that, I told a few close friends about my experience. Then I began to tell anyone I knew who was facing death, especially my many friends who were dying of AIDS. Now, sometimes I tell people in 12-step meetings about it when I tell my story. Otherwise, I am very private about it as some people think it's pretty bizarre. I read of Liz Dale's research, and it was incredible to know others had also gone through this.

Years after my near-death experience, I became a midwife. I felt that same sort of love and light present at the home births I attended, especially when the baby was having a tough time starting up. I felt that light or presence decided which way the life force went. Life and death—both ends of the tunnel were open—I felt it then. Now, as a nurse, I don't attend births. Being in a hospital is very boring by comparison. But midwifery was also very exhausting—feeling that turmoil. I wanted to exert pull for life, but I know I was only a vehicle; all my talents as a midwife did not decide the outcome—a Higher Force did. None of my mothers or babies died, but I knew they could easily have if it had been their time.

One time at a very normal birth at midwifery school, I suddenly left the room. While other midwives assisted the woman giving birth, I quietly gathered a small baby bath of ice cubes. About 10 minutes later, when all efforts to get the newborn to breathe had failed, the tub was there to shock the infant to life.

I had a close neighbor, Stan, who was dying of AIDS a few years ago whom I spoke with often about my NDE. It seemed to comfort him. About a year after he died, there was a terrible fire in our neighborhood. We had to wet down our roofs to try to save our homes. I was unable to get the water of an absent neighbor's home turned on which was very near the fire. I suddenly heard Stan's voice telling me how to connect hoses through the woods from our cabin. I don't know how that happened, but I do know it did not scare me. Maybe he came because we were connected by our conversations somehow.

About two years ago I was witness to a motorcyclist hit-and-run in the fast lane of the freeway just ahead of me. I remember realizing there was a person hit, then saying, "Let's go," as I stopped my car in the fast lane. I do not remember walking through two lanes of traffic on 101 to drag him to the side of the road and lay him out. I'm small, about 5'3". It really wasn't possible for me to do it. I felt a glow, a warmth. Only later did I begin to shake and have my teeth chatter. I guess this sounds odd, but I don't experience fear like I used to, not for myself.

I believe now that a non-sexual entity of all love exists for all time for all of us. I have felt it. We are watched over and guided and cared for always. We are never alone before or after death.

I believe I am supposed to aid people by telling them about what happened to me, especially those facing and fearing death. No one needs to fear this—we are all loved, guided, and waited for by a loving entity. We all have a "right" time to go to that light. I feel it's like an appointment. Those who accidentally or mistakenly try to go earlier have near-death experiences. I believe we are messengers to tell others the path is safe, loving, and nothing to fear.

Prior to my NDE my life was one of chaotic depression and self hatred. I only wanted to stop the pain and end my life. My life since has been a journey growing closer to the light, a sort of spiral. I am sure I am here for a purpose every day and feel a need to do service in my life. We are all works in progress. I feel I have been blessed to have this second chance to savor life and aid others while I'm here.

1. Did sexual identity come into play during your NDE?

No.

2. After the NDE, did the near-death experience change your sexual identify in any way or change the way you feel about your sexual identity?

Shortly after my NDE, after having "forgotten" it for 12 years, I remembered my first consensual sexual experience with another person, a girl my own age, where we had been caught "in the act" when I was 11 years old. I had been repressing the memory because of the trauma caused by other reactions to my sexual relationship with another girl. I suddenly knew I could not live lies for anyone else anymore. I felt relieved and scared all at once. It was like a window into my inner being had suddenly appeared and I felt lighter, excited and hopeful. It made sense of my life and my heart.

The first woman I fell in love with as an adult was in the same psychiatric system as I was. She killed herself later that year. The trauma of that experience affected me deeply. I still remember her today, 26 years later. However, slowly afterwards, I began to reach out again, knowing somehow I was on the right path.

A NEAR-DEATH CLOSET

Mark is a 45-year-old gay man living in, of all places, San Francisco.

I'm a fully accredited substitute school teacher, which in this day and age of teacher deregulation is quite unique. I enjoy my job and find it keeps me young. I'm also divorced after 18 years of being a "Domestic Partner." Sounds more like a cleaning service rather than a marriage.

First of all, the information I'll be sharing with you I don't readily share with people, especially strangers. Even those close to me regard what I consider an NDE with skepticism or slight amusement. It's as if I'm pushing some kind of religion on them, which is funny to me since I'm so against organized religions.

I was skiing at Kirkwood, California. It was 1990 and I was going down one of my favorite slopes which, when groomed, is nirvana. It's an advanced slope with some fairly steep parts. Anyway, I was halfway down when I decided to catch my breath. I stopped about a quarter of the way from the tree-lined boundary. As I looked up towards the peak I saw someone going almost straight down, in a long parabolic curve. I thought to myself I'd better move out of the way, just in case. I began to move

111

backwards into the crudded-up snow that delineated the boundary of the trail. I stopped and again looked up the hill. The person was coming right at me and I knew impact was inevitable. I hunched myself into a standing ball and heard an incredible, cracking crunch.

When I regained consciousness, I was up in the air. It was as if a string was holding me up through my center of balance. I remember seeing a surrealistically blue sky, the tops of the pine trees and part of the sun. I also felt the presence of a being. With this presence was a feeling of love, the magnitude of which cannot be expressed. I have never known such peace, contentment and most importantly, love. There was some kind of communion between it and myself. I don't know how long we were together. I remember thinking to myself, "Wow, this is really neat." It was at this point I felt the weight of my body (especially the weight of my feet in the ski boots) and came crashing down on my ass. So much for my "religious experience."

In retrospect, I do believe that I was close to some kind of death or death related experience. This being I was in communion with was God. What a content feeling, now knowing there is a God. So much for my agnostic past.

This was a God of absolute, unconditional love I communicated with. It had no sex or form. Does love have a gender or physical form on this our human plane? I know now that our spirits will continue when we "die" from this earthly form.

I've read a little about other people's experiences with this. I didn't have a tunnel or light experience. I didn't have a review of my life flash before me. I didn't think of loved ones, living or dead, during my experience. In fact, maybe it was a selfish experience—just me and this presence.

Previously, I'd always been afraid of dying. In 1984, I had a lover die of AIDS. It was horribly painful and ugly. By the end of those four months, I could run that ICU. If I could do it again, I would have been an intensive care unit nurse.

I'm no longer afraid of dying. I think that all people, no matter how evil and shitty they are, go back to this God. That's a beautiful feeling.

My spiritual life before my NDE was quite agnostic. I had and still have a marked disdain for most religions. Being gay, I find their bombastic, egocentric interpretations quite malevolent. It takes only a few of their "preachers" to spoil it for the whole. They pervert the truth on which their original tenets are based.

As I said, I had a lover die of AIDS in 1984. It was an ugly, painful death. I watched this beautiful, strong young man die over a four month period, most of which was in the intensive care unit. Since then, I was really scared of death. This changed totally when I had my NDE in 1989.

Since my NDE, as written in my experience, I'm no longer afraid of dying.

One author, P.M.H. Atwater, describe it best:

> *You know it's God.*
>
> *No one has to tell you.*
>
> *You know.*
>
> *You can no longer believe in God, for belief implies doubt.*
>
> *There is no more doubt. You now know God and you know that you know and you're never the same again."*

You know, it's hard to be a part of this unconditional love. There is so much animus in this world. How can one begin to nullify it? I guess you start with yourself. I now see, feel, communicate with God more often. I find communion with God in those things beautiful and inspiring to me: nature (*especially* nature), art, music, certain people. It can and does move one to tears, thus my private communication with God. And it's a sublime experience.

1. Did sexual identity come into play during your NDE?

No, not at all. Maybe if I went to a deeper, higher level (see Kenneth Ring's book) it *might* have been an issue.

2. After the NDE, did the near-death experience change your sexual identify in any way or change the way you feel about your sexual identity?

No, not at all.

CROWNED I

just dropped in to se
had been just "ex
day. Twice as
drowned i
backya
pulle

Steve was born in Dayton
children. He has lived in S
Vice President of the tour guides at Grace Cathedral.
Recently, he has started his own company, Cathedral Tours of
San Francisco! He gives docent-led walking tours of the
largest cathedrals in San Francisco.

On August 22, 1950, the day I was born my mother said she named me "Steven" because it meant Crowned in Heaven, not on Earth. After you read my story, you may agree my mom made a good choice for my name.

Unknown to my family, another baby boy had been born at the same hospital on August 17, 1950. We would become soul-mates, but not until we would meet in 1971 for the first time.

As a young boy, I seemed to have many more serious accidents than most kids. I'll quickly mention a few. In one accident, I got hit by a car which drove over me while I was on my bicycle. I came out without a scratch! Another time, I fell 18 feet from an acoustical ceiling in a bowling alley onto a wooden bowling lane. I blacked out when I started to fall. When I regained consciousness, my mother was crying. She was thinking I was surely going to die from the unbearable pain. I jokingly told my mom, "I

e her score." Like boys, my brother and I
ploring." The hospital released me the same
a child I almost drowned. Once I almost
the ocean, another time in a pool in a neighbor's
d. Both times I became unconscious. My brother
d me out.

I always figured I was lucky to be alive, but in my soul, I knew I had "Guardian Angels." I was very spiritual, even as a child. At about seven or eight, I heard a voice that asked me over and over again, "Who am I? Why am I here on Earth? What is my purpose?"

I always had a natural inclination to help people and to care for animals. I couldn't even put a worm on a hook. My dad called it being a "sissy." I knew it was love and respect.

Also, I had choked on food several times—to the point of becoming unconscious. When I was 14, my mom said, "I don't know how you make it through the day!"

In 1967, at the age of 17, I had an emergency appendectomy. No one knew until I was in surgery that my appendix had allowed poison to circulate throughout my entire system the day before. After the operation, I went into a coma and was told my coma lasted three months. (I've never checked with the hospital; maybe it was only a three-week coma.) Between the operation and waking up from my coma, I had a near-death experience. I wouldn't know there was a name for what I experienced—or that millions of other people had had one—until 1992 (twenty-five years later.) Most people float down a dark tunnel towards a light they know is a higher power. I didn't experience that. This is what happened to me.

My first realization was that I was floating stationary (not moving) in a warm, grayish cloud or mist. Slowly, six angels (or entities) appeared around me. I felt a great overwhelming feeling of peace, joy, and total non-judgmental acceptance and love for who I was. I had a body, but it was very light, almost weightless. I could see, but I had no face or eyes. Neither did they. We were all in robe-like clothing. None of us seemed to have feet or to touch the ground. There was no ground. I felt a great feeling from them, directed to me, that they all knew me and everything about me and my earthly life. It seemed that they were very pleased with me.

We exchanged thoughts by what I would call mental telepathy. Everything that happened there was instantaneous. I felt like I asked questions and they gave me answers. The second I had a question mentally, I had their answer (although there, it was totally non-material). No words were spoken. There was no "time" there. I could feel the sense and acceptance of "knowing" everything and eternity. There was no fear of anything because I knew the true answer to everything. I felt a knowledge that these six angels, or spiritual entities, were probably older relatives of mine who had gone on before me, but I wasn't clear who they were. I knew they were all good and positive "beings."

What is so difficult is to try to describe a spiritual place with earthly human words. How does one "see" without eyes? How could I "feel" without a body? I must have been a "spirit" to have done so. The last thing I recall was that they asked if I wanted to stay with them or if I wanted to come back to earth in my body. I wanted to stay with them, but they "sent" me back anyway. Years later, when I remembered, I was so angry when I realized they had "sent" me back. It was so beautiful when I felt the divine love. I had really wanted to stay.

I didn't realize I'd had a near-death experience until by chance I picked up a paperback copy in a bookstore of *Life After Life* by Dr. Raymond Moody. Reading the first person's NDE story sent chills from my head to my feet. I knew that what had happened to me was "real." It wasn't a dream. I knew that because dreams are fuzzy, confusing, out of order. My NDE was very clear, orderly, positive, good and beautiful. The feelings I experienced there were more real than feelings here on earth. I had been to a "level of heaven!"

Coming out of the hospital, every noise was unbearably loud. Daylight, even when overcast or cloudy, was blinding and actually hurt my eyes. Even now, years later, I can't stand bright lights at home, supermarkets, or in stores. I couldn't speak for over two weeks after I left the hospital. I had great difficulty walking, writing, eating and sleeping. I couldn't stand television, violence, radios, or movies. I had constant feelings of care and love. I knew in my spirit that every person was connected to everyone else, that we were and I was a part of the living trees, plants, flowers and oceans.

I knew that everything was and is united in this universe. I cried often for the state of our world: wars, hunger, people being killed. It was too much! If I saw a flower, its beauty was overwhelming and I would cry. (Sometimes I still do this, years later.) Going back to school in the seventh grade, I realized I didn't have to study like before, I automatically knew the answers, and I knew I was correct. I had a lot more energy. Even today, I have spontaneous, very quick head and body jerks which are uncontrollable.

At times, I feel like a jolt or bolt of lightening goes through me very fast. For over two years, if I wore a watch, it would stop running. At night I would play with the neighborhood kids in the street like we used to. If I walked under a streetlight it would go out. The kids would beg me to run from one end of the street to the other—they knew if I did, each streetlight would go out as I ran under it. If I came near a computer it would goof up or stop working. Everything and everyone became precious to me. All fear left me.

Also, I came back with an unquenchable desire to learn. I had to spend hours and hours in libraries. I read everything; I couldn't get enough, fast enough. I read about architecture and history. People's biographies fascinated me. I read very fast. I could comprehend by glancing. I loved and respected all peoples, cultures, all races. . . love, respect, and dignity. But I never felt better than other people. Actually, I felt humble.

In 1982, I was called spiritually to move to San Francisco, California from Ohio where I'd grown up. I moved in 1983 and stayed until 1984, when I returned to Ohio because my mother was terminally ill with breast cancer.

In 1982, I had a premonition—dreaming of a place. The dream was unmistakably clear, like I was awake. When I moved to San Francisco in 1983, I was invited to a New Year's Eve Party. Going there, I experienced exactly the place I'd experienced in my premonition. Chills hit me from head to toe. For me this meant I was in the right place here in San Francisco. My life became synchronized with my spirit. After my mother passed over to the spirit world in 1988 I moved back to San Francisco, and reside here presently.

I have since been saved from death by my "Guardian Angels" from a terrible auto accident. Driving on the freeway once, an audible voice told me, "Pull off the freeway immediately." As I sat in my car on the side of the road feeling a bit bewildered, I watched several cars pass me. To my horror, they crashed into an ammonia tanker truck, which had just seconds before fallen from the third and top level overpass onto our road.

I've also lost twenty of my closest friends I'd known for eighteen years to AIDS. But I "know" they're in a much better life. I know they help and guide me. I sometimes "feel" they are near me.

I have also experienced an astral projection with my soul-mate Jim in 1988, a year after his death from AIDS. He's the baby boy who was born in the same hospital as I, five days before me. He's one of my strongest guides (if I listen) and sometimes makes things happen to me that make me laugh. I know it's him.

Most people who have an NDE return with their personal lives changed but also return with a special purpose to carry out, given to them by their guide(s). The mission given to me was in three parts:

One is to tell people who are dying or those who have people who have already passed over to the other side that although their passing-over is difficult for us, there is truly nothing to fear. We should not fear death, because in reality none of us truly dies. We only shed our bodies like a butterfly sheds its cocoon, or like a snake sheds its skin. Our true selves, our spirits or souls, live on in a different spirit dimension or world. There is no death. I was told to tell others it makes no difference if you are religious or what your religion is. It makes no difference if have one or not. No matter who you are and no matter what you've done in your life, you are accepted into the spiritual dimension.

Second, fear is a man-made emotion that humans manufacture in place of "knowing" and "understanding" something. Fear is not real.

This may ruffle some feathers. Third, I would not tell you this if my spiritual entities or angels had not told me to tell this—be very careful of religious leaders or teachers who say that this person or that person will not get into heaven because they are this or that. This concept is very dangerous to claim or say and is used from a judgmental and false sense of self-morality. They said, "Very often the enemy of peace and holiness is not sin, but morality." The law of God is written in each of our hearts, so we need only to be true to ourselves and who we are. It is NO person's place to say whether or not anyone will or will not get into heaven. This is only for the highest power of the universe to decide. There are many pathways to God. There are pathways for Buddhist, Hindus, Taoist, Unitarians, and even those with no belief.

The judgment after we leave our earthly bodies and go to the spiritual dimensions is not a judgment of our lives by someone else. We see our lives on earth before us and learn from our mistakes, but there is no "judgment" on this spiritual level.

In closing, I will say that my near-death experience dramatically changed who I was and how I lived. I live not by what I read and "think" is right; I live by what I "know" is right for me. This doesn't mean it's right for you. I still go to church and worship God, but God doesn't *"need"* people to worship Him. One doesn't have to do anything to go to heaven.

I know also from my NDE that I have had several past lives. I personally believe in reincarnation. I've had many vivid dreams of past-life places which are very clear.

Also, I will mention that I have been HIV positive since 1985. It's now 1999. Except for a few physical ailments, I'm very healthy and have no fear of passing over. As a matter of fact, I will welcome it, because I know how wonderful it is.

We are here on earth to learn from each other and help each other. If we want to "learn," we must keep an open mind.

Just like everyone else here, I am not simply a human being. I am a spirit with a human shell. Someday I will leave my body and continue in the spiritual, non-material realm again.

In closing, I will bring those reading this to the present—October, 1999. I moved to San Francisco because of an inner-spiritual calling in 1995. I've been disabled—but appear to be completely healthy—although I've been HIV positive since 1985. I was diagnosed with heart problems last year and am on medication. Also, I have mild epilepsy at age 49.

I try to remain as active as possible by volunteering at Grace Cathedral in San Francisco. I am the Vice President of the Tour Guides. This has given me the opportunity to share my near-death experience with many people who come to the Cathedral for solace. This has led further into sharing my greatest gift with people in distress because a loved one has died or is enduring hardship. It is a joy for me to remind them that, although their loss is painful, in truth no one really dies. After death, people go into a spiritual dimension where they continue to live. Who is better than I to convey this? This new pathway is the most satisfying thing I've ever done.

I feel drawn now to speak to groups of people to lecture about my NDE. Through this, I've become very compassionate of others and have found the most truly satisfying mission of my life.

1. Did sexual identity come into play during your NDE?

Yes, only that as I was aware that I could see from a distance. I was surrounded by six spiritual (positive) entities (angels) floating in mid-air; I was also aware that it was definitely me in the center of them. My form was spiritual **male**, and also my physical **male** body combined. Even in spirit, I was **male**.

2. After the NDE, did the near-death experience change your sexual identify in any way or change the way you feel about your sexual identity?

Only that *before* I had my NDE, at the age of 17 years, I was not aware of what being gay was, or meant. I leaned later (about age 18 or 19) from friends. Most importantly, because my being a "gay" male was **not mentioned to me** by my six spiritual entities (or angels), there was nothing "wrong" about my being gay.

One of the most important lessons I learned in my NDE was that when I returned to earth and my regular life I was to tell other gays and lesbians that my spiritual entities knew everything about me, including my being gay. If being gay was something truly "wrong," my angels would have told me so. The constant reminders and harassment about being gays and lesbians by Christian fundamentalists and others ("because the Bible says so") are producing nothing but discord and misunderstanding.

If being gay or lesbian is such a horrible thing, I'm sure God's angels (my six spiritual guides) would have been told by God to tell me of my gay life being the "wrong" way to live. It was not mentioned or brought up in any way.

This changed me within myself—my own true spirit— to believe in myself and to treat myself with respect and dignity. The scriptures about homosexuality in the Bible by Paul are his writings in *Romans*. In the Scriptures, Jesus Christ didn't say with his own mouth or words that being homosexual is wrong. In all his preaching, Jesus never mentioned the topic of being gay or lesbian because, after all, it's not a big deal.

SHADOWY FIGURES

Born in Chicago, Illinois in 1931. Formal course of education in Catholic schools. Moved to California in 1961. Lived in Bay Area until July, 1999, when I moved to San Diego in southern California. An uneventful career as an office worker. Now retired and pursuing my hobby of gardening.

On Thursday morning, December 5, 1991, I left for work at 6:45 a.m. I worked at 2101 Webster Street in Oakland, California. The walk from my home would be perhaps 10 minutes, door to door. As I approached the corner of 23rd and Harrison, I noticed that I was breathing, but not getting any air. A car was parked on the sidewalk, so I put out my hand to steady myself. I was engulfed by waves of black. This was my second episode of pulmonary emboli. I was age 60 at the time of the experience.

I awoke between the car and the building and had been out for half an hour. My head was cradled on my left arm, and I was sprawled out on the pavement. I opened my eyes and saw the green of my windbreaker jacket, so I knew I was still in this world. I felt completely drained of energy and, with great effort, I pushed myself up with one arm into a semi-sitting position.

When I looked up, I was surrounded by shadowy figures, looking down at me. I could see the figures *and* I could see through them, like smoke or fog. I could see through them to the on-coming traffic on Harrison Street and the sun rising over the hills. The figures were looking down at me. They were tall and slender with narrow shoulders, heads like ET, wide temples and narrow jaws, but the features were indistinct. They were dressed in long capes which hung in thick folds to the ground. On their heads were Spanish-style hats with broad brims and shallow crowns. Somehow I was not surprised by them.

I was taking deep breaths and my heart gave a single heavy beat. The figures moved a few feet away. There was no sense of motion and the folds of their capes did not move. Another heart thump and the figures moved a few more feet away. Another heart thump and they moved into a formation, like a wedge: first one, then two in the next row, three in the last row. Again, there was no sense of motion. The capes remained still and I could see the traffic moving along on Harrison street. I noticed that the figures did not have feet. The cloaks just cleared the ground and there were stubs in place of feet. The figures were all looking up the street away from me except for the one in the third row on the left. It turned its head 180 degrees and looked at me. After every beat of my heart, the figures moved further away until they were at the corner of 24th and Harrison Street. They continued to move with each heartbeat, diagonally across the intersection of Harrison and Bay Place, to the Cadillac showroom. All this time, the figures had been moving on the sidewalks. But from Harrison and Bay Place, they seemed to angle upward into the rising sun. I had no messages from them. I saw no lights or visions. I heard nothing. I have not had a similar experience before or after. I was hospitalized for two and one-half weeks and consider myself blessed to have survived my second episode of pulmonary emboli.

My NDE did not notably affect my life after the experience. The experience did give me a greater perception of the texture of life and the tenuous relationships of the here-and-now and the hereafter. The two do seem to interest me, but only in the most subtly transparent manner.

1. Did sexual identity come into play during your NDE?

Sexual identity or sexual preference was not a factor in my NDE. In looking back on this experience, the shadowy figures surrounding me on my regaining consciousness would have taken me if my heart had not cleared itself of blood clots. In point of fact, my heart did give a big THUMP. I was breathing and getting oxygen and I survived.

Just before I collapsed, I noticed for a few seconds that I was breathing. That is, my lungs were going in and out, but I was not getting any air. There was no feeling of suffocation or being enclosed—just rapidly enveloping darkness.

If I had died, I think that the shadowy figures would have taken me—to where I do not know. With these figures, my personal identity was of no consequence to them. I was just a consignment to be claimed and taken away.

2. After the NDE, did the near-death experience change your sexual identify in any way or change the way you feel about your sexual identity?

The NDE did not change my concept of my identity, sexual or whatever. I am as I am. The experience was so impersonal. I can safely say NO CHANGE.

A WAKE-UP CALL

My name is Ed. I was a waiter in New Orleans, Louisiana at the time of my NDE in the mid 1970s. I was born in Brooklyn, New York in 1943. I now reside in San Francisco, California and am on disability. The change in my life has been more subtle than dramatic, but I will always be aware of my NDE.

Approximately 25 years ago in New Orleans, I was under the influence of alcohol and dexamils. I believe I overdosed and died, but for His reasons, God brought me back. From that day on, I know that our physical death is not the ending, but the beginning of something so great that it transcends our understanding which is limited to our finite five senses.

I floated out of my physical body which was on the bed and very slowly drifted toward the ceiling. At first, I felt a slight apprehension when separated from my body. Then, as I was inches from the ceiling of the room, a voice said, "It's not time yet." A calm came over me as I came back.

I have discussed this with my doctor. In his opinion, it was probably alcoholic hallucinations as I did drink heavily in those days. But I know what I experienced was an NDE. At the time, I didn't discuss it because people would not believe it. So I suffered in silence regarding my experience until I saw your article. That these "events" are being discussed in a non-judgmental manner has been a big help to me. I believe the NDE is a wake-up call to make us aware of God as we understand him and to give us a glimpse into the "beyond."

To explain this experience to a person who hasn't had one is tantamount to explaining the difference between red and green to a color blind person. It can't be done.

My experience was lying down in my bed and then my other self (soul) separated from my physical self and floated toward the ceiling. Before it went through the ceiling, a voice said, "It's not time yet." My "soul" then meshed with my physical body and I sat on the edge of the bed and said to myself, "I died and came back." A calm then overtook me.

Being able to tell my story has been the most positive thing that has happened since my experience. I believe it has made me stronger.

1. *Did sexual identity come into play during your NDE?*

No.

2. *After the NDE, did the near-death experience change your sexual identify in any way or change the way you feel about your sexual identity?*

It probably made me more accepting of my sexual orientation in later years.

So This Is How You Die

Phil was born of Irish immigrant parents and raised in San Francisco. He was a Catholic priest for 12 years. He married a former nun and has two grown children. He finally owned up to his "true self as a homosexual person" much to his present state of true serenity.

I am a 65 year old gay retired (1/18/99) psychotherapist of 33 years. On April 21, 1995 I underwent emergency quadruple bypass open heart surgery. Apparently I suffered an embolism during the surgery which caused a stroke in the right posterior lobe of my brain. This caused a traumatic mobile effect on my left hemisphere, especially my left arm and leg, with some residual damage to my speech capability.

Three days later, still in the hospital, I awoke during the night with four medics working on me to stabilize my heart as it had gone into a potentially lethal fibrillation. I was told I was in danger. The team kept verbally urging me to "Stay with them" and I would soon be stabilized.

During this time, thoughts flooded my mind as this was precisely the way my own father had suddenly died in 1970, after open heart surgery—fibrillation of his heart and death.

I began to think to myself, "So this is how you die. You just go unconscious and that's it." About that time, I had a picture in my mind of a very foggy night in rural Ireland with which I am very familiar. I was standing in a pasture surrounded by "stone fences."

Voices unknown to me kept urging me to "Go over. Go over."

I did not want to do so. I kept resisting and listening to one of the doctors injecting my arm saying, "Stay with me. You'll be ok. We've got you settled."

I was torn between the two requests being urgently made of me, but I did not want to "Go over!" Finally, I decided to look over the stone hedge to see, at least, what was there and there was nothing but a dense fog!

You decide!

1. Did sexual identity come into play during your NDE?

No.

2. After the NDE, did the near-death experience change your sexual identify in any way or change the way you feel about your sexual identity?

No.

LOOK TO THE STARS

Bryan is a 50 year old gay male who presently resides in Minnesota. He has continued his studies in holistics, metaphysics, and psychology. His NDE led him into a ten-year "reacquaintance" period with himself and only now, nearly 18 years later, does he feel ready to share his life with others in a more intimate and sexual sense. He is a waiter at present, but would like to someday become a psychologist, working especially in the area of dream interpretation.

> "From an endless dream we have come. In an endless dream we are living. To an endless dream we shall return!"
>
> —Kushi

When my NDE happened, my mother and father were with me. My mother cradled me in her arms and I went off into another place (they could find no pulse). This lasted only for a short while. The blood that was pouring from my bowels, nose, and mouth gave me a warm feeling. I was naked in a meadow. I was about 12 years old, healthy and tan. I was running with baby deer and monarch butterflies. There were lots of flowers, ferns and lush, green grass. There was also the feeling that anything that I loved, needed, or wanted was available to me nearby. I felt totally loved and relaxed, kind of like the very best of cuddling and sex. It was morning and everything was new and fresh. For some weird reason, I remember that I had every flavor of ice cream available to me. I also remember there were flavors that they've never even thought of. I soon became aware of those working on me and alas, became concerned, because I had made a mess of the lobby. Because I was all bloody and full of "stuff," I became concerned that the nurses might be gay. I was a mess—sad but true. "Make-overs" were not an option. Four days later, all the repair work broke loose and I ended up spewing blood all over my room again. I had insisted on getting up and being active. Since I was at Presbyterian Hospital in San Francisco, I was given a room overlooking the Golden Gate bridge. It was spectacular to watch the sunsets. I felt at peace.

During my experience, I went into meditation (since I am a person who meditates). When I opened my mind, I was in this meadow with golden light. I felt deep, deep peace. I am religious and there was a sense of God. He was a part of everything around me—the deer, the grass, the flowers— everything. There was only the sound of gentle breezes, no fear, no shame of being naked. I guess I felt like "Pan" or something. For some reason, I felt Greek in terms of nudity. The only message I received didn't come for some time. It was kind of like this is your experience with death and you will be spared from AIDS. I didn't even really know about AIDS in 1982.

After my NDE, I was hospitalized for 12 days and experienced two code blues. No one recognized the post-surgical depression. It was hard to get help. I ended up taking 12 valium for 12 days. This luckily snapped the depression and I went into a phase where for about five years I had no fear whatsoever of anything. I had "gotten" enlightenment and had also gotten clean and sober through Whitman-Radclyff in San Francisco. I was so impressed about being "in charge" of my own experiences! I studied, for example, *A Course In Miracles*, ZEN materials, Lazarus, Advocate Experience, and Integrity Training. I have the ability to channel in my writings—that is to say I can write in enlightenment jargon. I started to study things like crystals and all sorts of experimental New Age stuff. When I had my NDE I went into some sort of meditation and I was also spewing blood out of every orifice. My doctor said it was as if I was "exorcising myself" of demons. Ha! After the NDE, he and I talked a little about it, but my friends dismissed it as of no interest. I desired monogamous relationships more than ever (I have always been geared that way). I became much more open and unafraid to express my feelings and emotions. This scared off those I dated to some degree and I ended up facing the AIDS crisis since my NDE was in the summer of 1982. I had received 21 pints of blood but remain HIV-negative to this day. My frustration in dating and sex and my desire for romance, closeness, and sharing resulted in something like post-traumatic stress, exhibiting itself as OCD (obsessive compulsive disorder) and a tendency to go into panic. My life and finances started to fall apart around me as far as "externals" go. Everyone in the San Francisco gay community started dying. I was the one able to stand by and relate to everyone as they "passed" through various stages prior to death. I am gifted with compassion, but I ended up on disability due to medications for OCD, like klonopin and buspar, etc. Now I am in a really good phase, but the last two years were filled with psychiatric wards and, for some strange reason, delusions. I am on Luvox and Depakote. Now people in the gay community seem to use my new zest for life after the NDE to get me to work even harder for their own benefit. Since 1988, when everything fell apart, I haven't had sex, but I have a great ability to fantasize. I am very sexually active with me—ha! Since 1980, I have been writing poetry about all of this, and I am thinking of compiling some sort of book with my own original photos (I am gifted in that). I am discouraged with the gay community because I think they treat each other horribly. Reading the *B.A.R.*, one gets the (really stupid) impression that tricking and stuff is really still abundant. I am frustrated at being 49, because I think like about 32 (when the NDE happened). After being in intensive care, I have realized I am not the center of the universe.

Unfortunately, after living in San Francisco since 1977, I was not able to afford to live on disability ($626 a month). People in "gay A.A." kind of turned their backs on me because I was on psychotropic meds. They felt I did not need them. I tried constantly to quit taking them, which always resulted in delusions of some sort. So now I live in exile (ha!) with my brother and 10 others on a ranch overlooking the wine country. I wish I could experience loving again in the sense of having a lover and having sex back in my life. God definitely has some purpose since none of the 21 pints of blood was tainted. There is so much love inside me to "join" in giving to one other!

Since my experience, I tend to have "review" dreams of almost every interaction with anyone in my life. I do not really dream about the experience itself. I have a lot of "naked" dreams—not really sexual dreams. I guess they are kind of like acceptance dreams by people that I felt misunderstood by. There are also a lot of "maze" dreams which involve escaping from being entrapped.

It may sound strange, but I am able to converse with or at least "know" what animals are thinking. I am also extremely gifted at the Zen art of "becoming" what I am doing. But I am frustrated as hell by the fact that I don't fit in anywhere. I just love to set up "environments," that is to say people come to my space and feel comforted. My space keeps shrinking because of lack of funds. Money seems irrelevant and I am still searching for what I want to be when I grow up, and I am 49!

I went into delusions four years ago because I was living under large power lines (PG&E). I could "feel" energy flow all over my apartment complex. My OCD resulted in my having to "debunk" my building constantly by spinning around with crystals. I still cannot understand all of this, but I had to get out of Sacramento to be able to experience relief. My psychiatrist says not to think in the past. They blame it on stress, etc. but I am wondering why these questions are on this survey. My watch "froze" (computerized piece of complicated junk). Time seems irrelevant to me. I tend to "flow" with the seasons. I love nighttime, but have to watch and to remember to sleep and eat often.

I moved back to town near my birthplace in Minnesota in November, 1998. By 1999, I had a two bedroom, three-story town house (subsidized housing) for $79 a month. "Rebirth" has become a daily experience. I am still alone, searching for my "soul mate." I'm looking for a youthful guy who is joyous and unburdened by desires and expectations. I am self-sufficient and filled with dreams. . . . I "look to the stars!" I now realize the freedom of being gay and being able to fit in everywhere, away from the "zoo-like" conformity of the gay ghetto. I love you. I find you everywhere—from the "secret place" within your heart soul. Reach out with forgiveness, love, and joy into the farthest part of the universe. Into all your affairs—let your *light* shine!

> "To see a world in a grain of sand, and heaven in a wildflower, hold infinity in the palm of your hand, and eternity in an hour."

William Blake

My NDE brought me deeply in touch with the life force (Chi) in every living thing. Since 1982, I have involved myself in the study of Buddhism, meditation, yoga, and holistics in order to keep focused on the blessings of life. Though I find it hard to gain acceptance of my NDE in mainstream psychology, transpersonal (body-mind-soul) psychologists embrace it as a true "turning point" in my life. It is important for me to say that merely because you, the reader, are human, I experience love for you. Peace!

1. Did sexual identity come into play during your NDE?

My NDE reflected God's love for me. The most intense feeling of being totally, unconditionally loved and taken care of accompanied a sense of total joy and bliss. I was young, tan, healthy, running, jumping, playing with fawns, butterflies, and basically **all** of God's creation. I was naked, about twelve years old and part of everything around me. I am reminded of God's words, "These commandments I give to you, but the greatest commandment is that you **love** one another!" No part of my NDE in the slightest way reflected anything about my sexual identity. The message was clearly, "You are loved and cared for."

2. After the NDE, did the near-death experience change your sexual identify in any way or change the way you feel about your sexual identity?

I came away from my NDE with a renewed sense of relationship with all living things, with a renewed dedication to the beauty of "union," of commitment, of relationship. I have never been intrigued by one-night stands, impersonal sex, just "getting off." I now have an even deeper sense of longing, for a companion, a lover, a friend, sexual intimacy, and yes, even the desire for a soul mate. Perhaps, most importantly, I **love** myself more.

Yellow, black, white, brown; gay, straight, bisexual, transgender—God loves us all! The important thing is that we love one another!

DISCUSSION

Crossing Over And Coming Home is a collection of stories from the gay community that delineates the effects of the near-death experience. Approximately three years ago, thirty people generously contributed their stories to this first-of-its-kind study of the NDE within the gay/lesbian/bisexual/transgender community. As is well known in the NDE literature, heterosexuals have been extensively "studied"; their stories are widely available over the years since Raymond Moody's first publication. Why is a study of the gay community important? As Pamela Kircher wrote in the endorsement for the book:

> "People in the gay community have been so close to death on so many occasions since the onslaught of the AIDS epidemic that they have become the natural experts on NDEs in our time. Because they not only have had NDEs themselves, but are surrounded by other people who have had NDEs, these communities are becoming a prototype of what communities might be if we are actually aware of our own mortality and live from the values learned in an NDE."

Most people who have had NDEs mention the experience (sometimes called the dying experience) as an invaluable gift. After reading these stories, we are moved by the spiritual development involved. As Melvin Morse noted:

"This book is about the healing power of spiritual experiences. The tragedy of the AIDS epidemic contains in it these inspiring stories of love and spiritual understanding."

We are all going to die. This is a reality we are all familiar with. As far as being acutely aware of our own mortality, one of our authors writes:

"My spiritual development and personal development over the past several years since my experience have been my top priority. We are here on earth to celebrate life, to love and help one another, to tap into and use all of the gifts and talents our creator has endowed us with; i.e. pursuing our "mission" on earth and in the divine plan. Unconditional love with practical application on a daily basis (and "fruit of the spirit") is how we help ourselves evolve and touch other people's lives. Giving and receiving are fused together. We each have our own unique path, yet we are all on the same journey: conforming to the creator's likeness, day by day, and finally going home."

In the foreword, Melvin Morse writes:

"We will have a near-death experience when we die. The scientific research on NDEs clearly documents that NDEs are in fact the dying experience. Gay or straight, brown skin or white skin, or rich and poor alike, we will all have one when we die. Those who have had the dying experience and then lived often report that our lives are made meaningful by the loving relationships we form when we are alive."

This book is also important in that it addresses the negative influences that affect the gay community. Melvin Morse reminds us:

> ". . . the loving relationships that gay and lesbians forge during life are often discussed, trivialized, ridiculed, and even angrily denounced by society."

This lack of acceptance that permeates many cultures has a negative influence on all of us, gay and straight alike. It is imperative that we open our eyes to the fact that God (the Buddha, the Divine, the Spirit, Allah) loves all of us, regardless of our life styles. Globally, we are beginning to see an awareness of combating negativity, hatred and violence against the gay community.

One of the authors from *Crossing Over And Coming Home* discussed his experience on the other side and God's response to his gayness when he stated, "Is it okay to be GAY?" He was told, "Who do you think made gay people?" At that point the spirit guides and this author *began to laugh for what seemed like 1000 years*. He stated, "I felt like I fit in for the first time in my entire life. Completely fit in."

Elizabeth Kubler-Ross in *The Tunnel and The Light* wrote about thousands of people who had NDEs but were not willing to have their stories published. They were fearful that others would learn about their NDEs and felt that their experience was very personal, very private. We found this to be true of this group of gay authors as well. As PMH Atwater wrote:

> "For the individual, it is especially important that a comfortable climate exists for the sharing of their stories."

Approximately one-third of our gay-identified authors dropped out of this study when the decision was made to publish this book. Although we have their questionnaires and their stories, these authors preferred to remain fully anonymous.

In reviewing the questionnaires, a composite sketch was made in which the majority of the authors endorsed the following items:

- The majority did NOT have a tunnel experience (PMH Atwater predicted these findings)
- The majority experienced a presence of light
- They felt a comfort within the light and were not frightened by it
- They saw/experienced other beings or entities
- The light stayed with them during the NDE
- The majority did NOT have a life review
- They learned something new
- They found that their interest in spirituality changed (increased)
- They felt they had a positive experience
- The majority felt a sense of healing
- Questions were answered that had not been asked (mental telepathy)
- The majority did not have an angel with them
- The majority did not notice a change in their sexuality during the NDE.

We will now turn to some general themes from *Crossing Over And Coming Home* in relation to core concepts from various authors in the field. Many lessons can be gleaned from the thought provoking stories of Melvin Morse, MD, in *Closer To The Light*. Dr. Morse writes about his interest in researching the moment of death, which he refers to as the "point of death." He details the resistance from within the Seattle Medical Community when attempting to get funding for various NDE studies. The physician-researcher explains that he wanted to understand what his patients experienced "beyond the great divide." By way of illustration of his reference to point of death, we turn to *Crossing Over And Coming Home* for specific examples of *feeling states at the time of death*:

"I felt no pain at all, I felt completely whole and free...I saw my physical body all crumpled and bloody and lifeless and this enormous wave of compassion washed over me."

"My NDE happened as the result of a deliberate overdose in 1973. When I tried to kill myself, I was in deep despair and depression...I felt a tremendous feeling of rushing, speeding of myself towards a brilliant warm, white, sparkly light...I felt surrounded by the most intense peace that I had ever experienced."

"My heart rate accelerated. I began to sweat, and then to feel chilly, as my blood pressure fluctuated. I began to see flashes of various periods of my life...I could feel my heart throbbing in my chest..."

"I remember being amazed that I was not frightened; I had always thought it would be frightening to die. I felt amazingly calm as I watched my mother; I felt such pain for her...Now I realize dying can be peaceful and non-terrifying."

From the perspective of *thought processes* that occur at the "point of death," our study participants reported:

"I suddenly believed that I could have a life of less pain—that I did not have to die to have no pain...I knew that death itself wasn't painful to the body. I realized there was something after death. I knew I was not supposed to choose my time of death."

"My thoughts of vengeance towards the hospital gave way to thoughts that I did not want to leave this world with such negative energy consuming my consciousness...it was pureness of heart, a fine, bright flame of compassion, a thread of pure gold, that was left after my transfiguring experience."

"I learned that plans existed for me and that I had altered those plans by suicide. I could (or must?) go back. There was much to do. I remember not exactly wanting to leave, but not resisting, either. Having seen the other side, I complied agreeably somehow and was imported with these last words: 'Show them the way.'"

From a *behavioral* or action-oriented way, some examples of "point of death" follow:

"The experience was so deep, intense, and powerful I crumpled to my knees then fell on the floor with tears of joy in my eyes. My body/spirit could not handle any more of this overpowering immersion. It was like a 220 current frazzling a 110 socket. It almost became unbearable, the huge wave after wave of exquisite joy, communion, presence of the divine fused with a limited human being…"

"The darkness is all about me. There is no place to run. I am aware of all, but I do not have any physical movements, no energy to move, whether motor activity or animation. I am frozen in place."

Ken Ring in his recent book *Lessons From the Light* wrote about the *self-evidentiality of an afterlife*. One chapter of the book gives numerous examples of people who have come back to report "with rock-solid conviction" that an afterlife truly does exist. Here are some examples from our gay-identified study that exemplify this point:

"I realized life was about risk and openness and honesty. I had been afraid for years of the labels lesbian and gay…I believe now that a non-sexual entity of all love exists for all time for all of us…we are watched over and guided and cared for always. We are never alone before or after death…I believe we are messengers to tell others the path is safe, loving and nothing to fear."

"This was a God of absolute, unconditional love I communicated with. It had no sex or form. Does love have a gender or physical form on this our human plane? I know

now that our spirit will continue when we "die" from this earthly form."

"I believe I overdosed and died, but for "His" reasons, God brought me back. From that day on I know that our physical death is not the ending, but the beginning of something so great that it transcends our understanding which is limited to our finite five senses."

"(At death) we only shed our bodies like a butterfly sheds its cocoon…there is no death…"

Raymond Moody, in *Life After Life* writes about the *effect of light* on the near-death experience. In correlating his work with our gay population, we offer the following examples:

"I felt like I was floating in a void of lightness and it felt peaceful."

"I am an ancient soul in a new body. I am an ancient soul on a forever journey towards the light in a new body, able to acknowledge those around me and recognize them as new or old souls."

"I slowly climb higher and higher towards this light. I must reach this light before it is too late, too late for what? I don't know. I am at peace, floating towards a light that is more essential to me than anything else that I reach out for."

"In November, 1995, I drove into a wall. I remember as my jaw hit the steering wheel, I said, "Oh shit! I'm dead!" and then I was…I was surrounded by light so intense I could feel it. I could not look, it just sort of permeated me."

"My NDE happened as the result of a deliberate overdose in 1973. When I tried to kill myself, I was in deep despair and depression…I felt a tremendous feeling of rushing, speeding of myself towards a brilliant warm, white, sparkly light…I felt surrounded by the most intense peace that I had ever experienced."

"I became separate from my body and floated to the ceiling. I looked down at the body stretched across the table and I realized it was my body. I then became four or five years old and floated straight up in an incredible light that surrounded me softly. It was like sunlight and smoke-like mist filled the room with the smell of roses."

Chris Carson, in *When Ego Dies*, wrote in the epilog about *love and fearlessness* which are tools we can use to navigate throughout life. Our gay-identified subjects relate the following examples of love and fearlessness:

"I am in the darkness alone but not afraid."

"There was no fear of anything because I knew the true answer to everything."

"I do not remember struggling or being afraid. I felt only deep peace and happiness."

"The feeling of love and peace was everything I ever wanted. I was truly home."

"I experienced seeing in all directions at once—the blackest sky with billions of the brightest stars in all directions. I was more "conscious" than I had ever felt before, but had no body. The people I saw…each welcomed me with a message of love and welcome, peace and happiness, but with no words…"

"I believe we are messengers to tell others the path is safe, loving, and nothing to fear."

"Fear is a manmade…emotion that humans manufacture."

"Positive changes, I believe, including my intelligence, openness to new ideas and change, no fear at all, naïve and simple."

"Until my late 20s, I was aware of a black hole in my center, never telling anyone about it until my 50s. Whenever I would become aware of it, I felt great fear. Now I believe that the black hole was near-death, which for me has been the most beautiful and peaceful experience in my life."

PMH Atwater in *Beyond The Light* writes about the NDE and the transcendent experience which she describes as ". . . *an exposure to otherworldly dimensions and scenes beyond the individual's frame of reference* . . . seldom personal in context . . . a mind-stretching challenge."

A variety of quotes from our study follows:

"My spiritual development and personal development over the past several years since my experience has been my top priority in my life. Learning about our divine dialogue and personal relationship is a key commitment and focus. We are here on this earth to celebrate life, to love and to help one another, and to tap into and use all of the gifts and talents our creator has endowed us with."

"I realize that someone or something (I call God or Goddess) has a special understanding of each of us, has plans for each of us that we need to carry out to be fully realized.

"I know that our physical death is not the ending, but the beginning of something so great that it transcends our understanding which is limited to our finite five senses.

"My near-death experience made me feel like I had a purpose here on earth, a destiny, that I had not yet fulfilled. It made me feel important."

"In this experience, I have learned I have a purpose, something important I'm supposed to do for society…today, I am a teacher and it feels like I am where I'm supposed to be. I fight injustice daily and teach kids to respect each other. I feel like I'm doing my part to 'heal the world'."

In conclusion, I hope you have gained some new knowledge and spiritual benefit from reading about the gay near-death experiences. Our group will be working on larger NDE studies for the gay community in the near future. We plan on a two-fold approach:

The gay NDE study will be available through all national and international IANDS Chapters and various gay centers in each of these locations.

The gay NDE study will be available on a new website specifically available for collecting our stories, sharing our experiences, coming out spiritually to each other about the effects of the NDE as well as other non-ordinary states of consciousness. On the internet, go to NDERF.ORG.

The most appropriate way to end this work of love is to quote from Elizabeth Kubler-Ross in *The Tunnel and The Light*:

"Here we will know that the absolute only thing that matters is love. Everything else, our achievements, degrees, the money we made, how many mink coats we had is totally irrelevant. It will also be understood that what we do is not important. The only thing that matters is how we do what we do and the only thing that matters is that we do what we do with love. In this total, unconditional love we will have to review not only every deed of our live, but also every thought and every word of our total existence. And we will have all knowledge. That means that we will know how every thought, word and deed, and choice of our total lives has affected others. Our lives areliterally nothing but a school, where we are tested, where we are put through the tumbler. And it is our choice, and no one else's choice, whether we come out of the tumbler crushed or polished."

APPENDICES

APPENDICES

I. Appendix A

Consent Form
Questionnaire

II. Appendix B

Appendix B covers the ten sections of the questionnaire. Each area has been analyzed using descriptive statistics. A few quotes have been added to clarify certain points. The questionnaire was my own design. I began reading about NDEs several years ago and began to organize the experience into distinct sections. A near-death experience may fall into some of these categories or may

I

be vastly different. I left a great deal of room within the questionnaire for each participant to explain any similarities or differences they had. An area at the end of each section was left blank for comments.

Appendix B also covers the participants' specific stories attached to the study questionnaire. Each story was analyzed in detail for themes that allowed for content analysis. PMH Atwater was kind enough to send along a guide she has used to analyze over 3,000 NDE stories. This information was compared to our gay NDE population for similarities and differences along with information gathered by the structured questions. Some final comments specific to this population have been added.

III. Appendix C

Appendix C covers specific aspects of analysis of NDE stories. Analysis covers common themes of the 21 NDE stories broken down into the following areas of study:

1) Thought processes
2) Feeling states
3) Behavioral manifestations
4) Overall effect of the NDE

I. Appendix A:
Consent Form / The Questionnaire

PLEASE SEND TO:

Liz Dale, Ph.D., RN
1316A Solano Avenue
Albany, CA 94706
510-526-7530

I, _____ give permission to **Liz Dale, Ph.D., RN**, to use the information I have presented to her in this questionnaire. I understand that this research project is not funded and that my participation is voluntary. I further understand that this research project is fully confidential. No specific biographical identifiers will be used. I further understand that I will be given a copy of the final report before publication. Should any direct quotes or specific identifiers be indicated, I will be contacted for specific consent before its use.

Signed_____

Date _____

QUESTIONNAIRE ON THE NDE
IN THE GAY COMMUNITY

PLEASE SEND TO:

Liz Dale, Ph.D., RN
1316A Solano Avenue
Albany, CA 94706
510-526-7530

Your Name _____   _____ Male
Address _____   _____ Female
City/State/Zip _____ _____ Gay/Lesbian
Phone # _____   _____ Bisexual
                                                 _____ Transgendered

Dear Fellow NDE'ers:

This is the FIRST NDE questionnaire of the gay community. Please complete the questionnaire as completely as possible and send it to me at the address above ASAP. All the information is confidential. No names or identifiers will be used in the final results. But, I would like to have your name, address, and phone should I have any questions about your responses. My intention for this research is to have the gay community represented in the NDE literature. Thank you in advance for your participation. Look for the results to be published in the BAR (BAY AREA REPORTER), a San Francisco free newspaper for gay community.

A Few Definitions:

Near-death experience refers to the phenomenon that occurs when a person clinically dies, leaves their body, and when revived, returns to his/her body.

For this study, gay community refers to gay, lesbian, bisexual, and transgendered people.

General Items

(circle yes or no)

Did you have a near-death experience	yes	no
Did it change your life in any way(s)	yes	no
Did it affect your life in any positive way(s)	yes	no
Did you discuss the NDE with other people	yes	no
Did your NDE affect your relationship(s)	yes	no
Did it affect your life in any negative way(s)	yes	no
Did the NDE affect your sexuality	yes	no

Describe the events that occurred at the exact moment of your death in this space or on the back.

The Tunnel

(circle yes or no)

Did your NDE include a tunnel experience	yes	no
Did you pass through darkness in the tunnel	yes	no
Was there any sound associated with it	yes	no
Were you pulled through the tunnel	yes	no
Were there other people or animals involved	yes	no
Did you feel peaceful in the tunnel	yes	no
Did you experience a sort of healing	yes	no
Did you merge with the light	yes	no
Did you feel an element of love	yes	no
Did you share your love with anyone	yes	no
Did you hear music in the tunnel	yes	no
Did you pass through lightness	yes	no
Did you meet a religious or spiritual leader	yes	no
Did you feel fear in the tunnel	yes	no
Did you have any questions come to mind in the tunnel	yes	no
Were any questions answered that you did not ask	yes	no

Please explain any of the above items here and/or on the back.

Did the people (entities) you met in the tunnel talk with you, give you instructions or some message? Explain here and/or on the back.

The Light

(circle yes or no)

Did you experience the presence of light	yes	no
Was the light the same as light on earth	yes	no
Did you feel a comfort within the light	yes	no
Did you feel frightened by the light	yes	no
Did you move through the light	yes	no
Did a light emanate from you	yes	no
Did a light emanate from others	yes	no
Did you merge with others in the light	yes	no
What was the color of the light (describe) _____		

Please explain any of the above items here and/or on the back.

Other Objects - Once Out Of The Tunnel

(circle yes or no)

Did you experience other people in the NDE	yes	no
Did you see or experience animals	yes	no
Did you see or experience other beings/entities	yes	no
Did the light stay with you once out of the tunnel	yes	no

Please explain any of the above items here and/or on the back.

The Angels

(circle yes or no)

Did you have an angel with you in the NDE	yes	no
Did an angel talk with you	yes	no
Did an angel offer you advice	yes	no

Describe your angel

Describe any advice given (whether verbal or just sensed)

Life Review

(circle yes or no)

Did you have a life review in the NDE	yes	no
Did you see yourself at an earlier age	yes	no
Did you see yourself with other people/entities	yes	no
Did other people/beings talk with you about your life	yes	no
Did you see yourself or others living in the future	yes	no

Describe any of the above in detail here and/or on the back

Your Dreams Since the NDE

Describe any changes in your dream life since the NDE, if any

Do you ever dream about your NDE?

Space Travel

(circle yes or no)

Did you travel to some other location in the NDE	yes	no
Did you spend time with other people	yes	no
Did you recognize the people you visited	yes	no
Did you converse with other beings	yes	no
Did other people talk with you	yes	no
Did you encounter any animals in your space travel	yes	no
Did you travel in a vehicle	yes	no
Did you move about more easily than you do on earth	yes	no

Explain any of the above questions here and/or on the back

Lessons Learned

(circle yes or no)

Did you learn something new in your NDE	yes	no
Did your interest in spirituality change	yes	no
Did other people think you had changed after the NDE	yes	no
Have you sought assistance in some way since the NDE	yes	no
Have you noticed a change in your energy level	yes	no
Have you attended any groups associated with IANDS*	yes	no

* International Association for Near-Death Studies

Describe any of the above in detail here and/or on the back

Life After The NDE

(circle yes or no)

Are you more sensitive to light or sound	yes	no
Do you have difficulty with your wrist watch	yes	no
Did your IQ change since the NDE	yes	no
Do you share your NDE experience with other people	yes	no
Do you have problems with electricity	yes	no
Do you have problems with electromagnetic fields	yes	no
Did you have difficulty reintegrating after the NDE	yes	no

Describe any of the above in detail here and/or on the back

II. APPENDIX B:
ANALYSIS OF THE QUESTIONNAIRE

Appendix B covers the 10 specific areas of interest from the questionnaire. Each area covered has been coded either yes, no, or ?.

A ? means the person answered yes *and* no, or left the question blank. A few common themes from each content area have been added for completeness.

Appendix B covers:

    A. General items
    B. The tunnel
    C. The light
    D. Other objects
    E. The angels
    F. Life review
    G. Your dreams since the NDE
    H. Space travel
    I.   Lessons learned
    J.   Life after the NDE

A. General Items

Did you have a near-death experience?	19 Yes	0 No	0 ?
Did it change your life in any way(s)?	18 Yes	1 No	0 ?
Did it affect your life in any positive way(s)?	18 Yes	1 No	0 ?
Did you discuss the NDE with other people?	18 Yes	0 No	1 ?
Did your NDE affect your relationship(s)?	13 Yes	6 No	0 ?
Did it affect your life in any negative way(s)?	8 Yes	10 No	1 ?
Did the NDE affect your sexuality?	5 Yes	12 No	2 ?

B. The Tunnel

Did your NDE include a tunnel experience?	7 Yes	11 No	1 ?
Did you pass through darkness in the tunnel?	10 Yes	8 No	1 ?
Was there any sound associated with it?	6 Yes	13 No	0 ?
Were you pulled through the tunnel?	7 Yes	12 No	0 ?
Were there other people or animals involved?	10 Yes	9 No	0 ?
Did you feel peaceful in the tunnel?	11 Yes	6 No	2 ?
Did you experience a sort of healing?	12 Yes	7 No	0 ?
Did you merge with the light?	6 Yes	11 No	2 ?
Did you feel an element of love?	14 Yes	3 No	2 ?
Did you share your love with anyone?	6 Yes	11 No	2 ?
Did you hear music in the tunnel?	2 Yes	15 No	2 ?
Did you pass through lightness?	8 Yes	8 No	3 ?
Did you meet a religious or spiritual leader?	9 Yes	7 No	3 ?
Did you feel fear in the tunnel?	1 Yes	15 No	3 ?
Did you have any questions come to mind in the tunnel?	5 Yes	12 No	2 ?
Were any questions answered that you did not ask?	10 Yes	9 No	0 ?

C. The Light

Did you experience the presence of light?	14 Yes	4 No	1 ?
Was the light the same as light on earth?	1 Yes	15 No	3 ?
Did you feel a comfort within the light?	14 Yes	4 No	1 ?
Did you feel frightened by the light?	1 Yes	17 No	1 ?
Did you move through the light?	10 Yes	8 No	1 ?
Did a light emanate from you?	8 Yes	10 No	1 ?
Did a light emanate from others?	8 Yes	10 No	1 ?
Did you merge with others in the light?	5 Yes	13 No	1 ?
What was the color of the light?	4 Yes	7 No	8 ?

D. Other Objects—Once Out of the Tunnel

Did you experience other people in the NDE?	10 Yes	7 No	1 ?
Did you see or experience animals?	3 Yes	15 No	0 ?
Did you see or experience other beings/entities?	9 Yes	8 No	1 ?
Did the light stay with you once out of the tunnel?	9 Yes	6 No	3 ?

E. The Angels

Did you have an angel with you in the NDE?	5 Yes	11 No	3 ?
Did an angel talk with you?	5 Yes	10 No	4 ?
Did an angel offer you advice?	5 Yes	11 No	3 ?

F. Life Review

Did you have a life review in the NDE?	4 Yes	12 No	3 ?
Did you see yourself at an earlier age?	8 Yes	10 No	1 ?
Did you see yourself with other people/entities?	7 Yes	12 No	0 ?
Did other people/beings talk with you about your life?	3 Yes	16 No	0 ?
Did you see yourself or others living in the future?	5 Yes	12 No	2 ?

G. Your Dreams Since the NDE

A. Describe any changes in your dream life since the NDE, if any.

_____

_____

_____

B. Do you ever dream about your NDE experience?

_____

_____

_____

H. Space Travel

Did you travel to some other location in the NDE?	9	Yes	10	No	0	?
Did you spend time with other people?	7	Yes	11	No	1	?
Did you recognize the people you visited?	5	Yes	12	No	2	?
Did you converse with other beings?	7	Yes	10	No	2	?
Did other people talk with you?	6	Yes	10	No	3	?
Did you encounter any animals in your space travel?	2	Yes	17	No	0	?
Did the animals communicate with you?	2	Yes	16	No	1	?
Did you travel in a vehicle?	1	Yes	18	No	0	?
Did you move about more easily than you do on earth?	13	Yes	6	No	0	?

I. Lessons Learned

Did you learn something new in your NDE?	18	Yes	1	No	0	?
Did your interest in spirituality change?	16	Yes	2	No	1	?
Did other people think you had changed after the NDE?	9	Yes	7	No	3	?
Have you sought assistance in some way since the NDE?	8	Yes	8	No	3	?
Have you noticed a change in your energy level?	4	Yes	9	No	6	?
Have you attended any groups associated with IANDS[*]	4	Yes	10	No	5	?

*International Association for Near-Death Studies

J. Life After the NDE

Are you more sensitive to light or sound?	15	Yes	3	No	1	?
Do you have difficulty with your wrist watch?	5	Yes	12	No	2	?
Did your IQ change since the NDE?	3	Yes	5	No	11	?
Do you share your NDE experience with other people?	16	Yes	2	No	1	?
Do you have problems with electricity?	7	Yes	10	No	2	?
Do you have problems with electromagnetic fields?	7	Yes	8	No	4	?
Did you have difficulty reintegrating after the NDE?	11	Yes	7	No	1	?

A. Analysis of General Items (N=19)[1]

100%	Did you have a near-death experience?
94%	Did it change your life in any way(s)?
94%	Did it affect your life in any positive way(s)?
94%	Did you discuss the NDE with other people?
68%	Did your NDE affect your relationship(s)?
42%	Did it affect your life in any negative way(s)?
26%	Did the NDE affect your sexuality?

Comments:

—NDE had positive effects, opened up world of spirituality.
—Everything changed...most people don't understand.
—A slight apprehension when separated...is a positive thing in my life now.
—Some depression about wanting to be there now.
—NDE was a peak experience.
—I was afraid they would think I'm crazy so I kept it secret.
—I started to study things like crystals.
—Positive changes including my intelligence, openness to new ideas, no fear.
—It made me feel like I had a purpose here on earth.
—I realized dying could be peaceful and non-terrifying.

B. Analysis of The Tunnel (N=19)

36%	Did your NDE include a tunnel experience?
52%	Did you pass through darkness in the tunnel?
31%	Was there any sound associated with it?
36%	Were you pulled through the tunnel?
52%	Were there other people or animals involved?
57%	Did you feel peaceful in the tunnel?
63%	Did you experience a sort of healing?
31%	Did you merge with the light?
73%	Did you feel an element of love?
31%	Did you share your love with anyone?
10%	Did you hear music in the tunnel?
42%	Did you pass through lightness?
47%	Did you meet a religious or spiritual leader?
25%	Did you feel fear in the tunnel?
26%	Did you have any questions come to mind in the tunnel?
52%	Were any questions answered that you did not ask?

---

1. Only nineteen of twenty-one subjects sent completed questionnaires. All twenty-one subjects sent their stories of the NDE.

Comments:

—I flew through space to the other side, no tunnel.
—I was half in light, half in daylight…the golden light and rainbow.
—I guess I didn't go far enough for a tunnel or light experience.
—I was aware of being taken care of, watched over.
—Tunnel was a street lined with trees.
—I experienced seeing in all directions at once.
—I realized every day afterwards, I was chosen to live.
—I was drawn along a wide expansive void.
—The only real message I received…you'll be spared from AIDS.
—I felt an incredible happiness and peace and excitement when being in the light.
—In the tunnel I felt surrounded by souls who loved me.
—I did not experience a tunnel, but went straight up into an incredible light.

C. Analysis for the Light (N=19)

73%	Did you experience the presence of light?
5%	Was the light the same as light on earth?
73%	Did you feel a comfort within the light?
05%	Did you feel frightened by the light?
52%	Did you move through the light?
42%	Did a light emanate from you?
42%	Did a light emanate from others?
26%	Did you merge with others in the light?
21%	What was the color of the light?

Comments:

—Color was other worldly, bright yet deep, fuller.
—Brightest white light I ever saw.
—In the tunnel, were talking about home.
—The light was billions of the brightest stars in all directions.
—Various degrees of white.
—No color, warm white-yellow, sparkly.
—I played in the light, I ran, danced, played.
—Light was an intense incredibly beautiful light.
—Light was like moon light…bluish light.
—The light was stark white combined with sunlight and smoke-like mist.
—Didn't really have a color, was just very light (white/yellow/gold).

D. Analysis of Other Objects (N=18)

55%	Did you experience other people in the NDE?
17%	Did you see or experience animals?
50%	Did you see or experience other beings/entities?
50%	Did the light stay with you once out of the tunnel?

Comments:

—I didn't see who I was talking to.
—Other people/entities/animals were familiar, but unidentifiable.
—I saw my father before this happened, he was upset with me.
—I sensed the guide was male, communicated telepathically.
—It's still with me, increases as I meditate on love and healing.
—The sense of God stays with me to this day.

E. Analysis of the Angels (N=19)

26%	Did you have an angel with you in the NDE?
26%	Did an angel talk with you?
26%	Did an angel offer you advice?

Comments:

—(Angel was) a young girl about 17 in Slavic peasant dress.
—Entities seemed to be angels, bigger and taller than me.
—Eyes were dreamy, shiny, beautiful people.
—Someone or something (communicated), a voice, all loving.
—There was another presence (stated) be at peace, you are loved.
—Something told me it wasn't time yet, I wasn't done, have more to do.
—Male, I think, did not see...advice was 'show them the way.'

F. Analysis of Life Review (N=19)

21%	Did you have a life review in the NDE?
42%	Did you see yourself at an earlier age?
36%	Did you see yourself with other people/entities?
15%	Did other people/beings talk with you about your life?
26%	Did you see yourself or others living in the future?

Comments:

—Saw myself at an earlier age, maybe 5 or 6 years of age with my mother who had died four years earlier.
—They walked me right through life.
—I felt the hands of a number of people, guiding me.
—I felt free and a sense of justice was all around.

G. Analysis of Dreams Since the NDE

Comments:

—Since NDE, increased health, increased awareness, unafraid
—One NDEr has many more vivid dreams, including astral projection
—More vivid, greater frequency
—Acceptance dreams by people I felt misunderstood by
—Many nightmares after NDE
—Change in dreams, very cautious of others and relatives
—I stopped flying in my dreams, before I used to drift out

H. Analysis of Space Travel (N=19)

47%	Did you travel to some other location in the NDE?
57%	Did you spend time with other people?
26%	Did you recognize the people you visited?
36%	Did you converse with other beings?
31%	Did other people talk with you?
10%	Did you encounter any animals in your space travel?
10%	Did the animals communicate with you?
5%	Did you travel in a vehicle?
31%	Did you move about more easily than you do on earth?

Comments:

—Danced effortlessly with mother in a field.
—Talked with people-no lips moved-sensed.
—Floating weightlessly…no boundaries.
—Just like the twilight zone.
—I am (now) able to know what animals are thinking.
—I moved from the river bottom to the top of the trees effortlessly.
—I sensed others with me and love and caring.
—I floated without weight and pain; kind of like bouncing effortlessly.

I. Analysis of Lessons Learned (N=19)

94%	Did you learn something new in your NDE?
84%	Did your interest in spirituality change?
47%	Did other people think you had changed after the NDE?
42%	Have you sought assistance in some way since the NDE?
21%	Have you noticed a change in your energy level?
21%	Have you attended any groups associated with IANDS?

Comments:

—I was reconnected to my mother, now in alternative therapy field.
—Learned that life in the present moment is most precious.
—Now interested in all religions and in spirituality.
—NDE showed a lot of future stuff…things that aren't happening now.
—Learned that I have to be careful of other people thinking I'm crazy.
—Learned not to fear death, learned I could leave my body.
—I learned I have a purpose, I'm supposed to do something important for society.
—I learned that God loves me just the way I am and I am learning to love myself.

J. Analysis of Life After the NDE (N=19)

The majority of NDErs are:

78%	Are you more sensitive to light or sound?
26%	Do you have difficulty with your wrist watch?
15%	Did your IQ change since the NDE?
84%	Do you share your NDE experience with other people?
36%	Do you have problems with electricity?
36%	Do you have problems with electromagnetic fields?
57%	Did you have difficult reintegrating after the NDE?

Comments:

—I shared my experience with only 2 or 3 people and they said I was crazy.
—I told Mom, but my dad believed me and friends do.
—I could feel energy flow all over my apartment complex
—I published two books on electricity.
—Wrist watch has to be waterproof or it keeps stopping.
—Only share NDE with people who might appreciate.
—Problems with light and sound.
—Took years before I began sharing story.
—There is no time, just now.

III. APPENDIX C:
THE STORIES ANALYZED

Appendix C covers specific aspects of NDE stories, grouped into the following themes:

1)   Thought processes
2)   Feeling states
3)   Behavioral manifestations
4)   Overall effects of the NDE

Thought processes are defined as thinking, meditation, reflection, conceived ideas, forming concepts, concentration, imagination.

Feeling states can be defined as sensing, subjective reactions, experiences perceived through the senses, and awareness.

Behavioral manifestations include actions, the way a person interacts, conducts themselves, responds to a stimuli or experience.

Overall effects of the NDE summarizes generalized effect of the NDE on a person's life, clarification of life's purpose, spiritual aspects, deeper meaning, and lessons learned.

Examples of Thought processes:

I consider myself blessed to have survived my second episode of pulmonary embolism.

Profound, ecstatic, transformative spiritual experience with the creator.

I was told, "You're going home…" yet I 'knew' it was my *real* home, not here.

I am an ancient soul in a new body. I am an ancient soul on a forever journey towards the light in a new body, able to acknowledge those about me and recognize them as new or old souls…I seek out to be near those who are old souls who are like me, whom I feel comfortable around without having to justify my existence to them.

We exchanged thoughts, by what I would call mental-telepathy. Everything that happened there was instantaneous. I felt like I asked questions and they gave me answers, but the second I had a question mentally, I had the answer…no words were spoken. There was no "time" there. I could feel the sense and acceptance of "knowing" everything and eternity.

I came back with an unquenchable desire to learn. I had to go and spend hours and hours in libraries. I read everything. I couldn't get enough, fast enough.

I experienced seeing in all directions at once—the blackest sky with billions of the brightest stars in all directions. I was more "conscious" than I had ever felt before, but had no body. The people I saw…each welcomed me with a message of love and welcome, peace and happiness, but with no words.

I suddenly believed that I could have a life of less pain—that I did not have to die to have no pain…I knew that death itself wasn't painful though dying itself can be painful to the body. I realized there was something after death. I knew I was not supposed to choose my time of death.

My thoughts of vengeance towards the hospital gave way to thoughts that I did not want to leave this world with such negative energy consuming my consciousness…it was pureness of heart, a fine, bright flame of compassion, a thread of pure gold that was left after my transfiguring experience.

When my NDE happened, my mother and father were with me. I was in a meadow naked, about 12 years old, healthy and tan, running with baby deer and monarch butterflies. There were lots of flowers, ferns and lush, green grass. There was also the feeling that anything that I loved, needed, or wanted was available to me, close-by…fresh.

Three days later, still in the hospital, I awoke during the night with four paramedics working on me to stabilize my heart as it had gone into potentially a lethal fibrillation and I was told I was in danger. The team kept verbally urging me to "stay with them" and I would soon be stabilized. During this time, thoughts flooded my mind as this was precisely the way my own father had suddenly died in 1970, after open heart surgery—fibrillation of his heart and death. I began to think to myself, "So this is how you die. You just go unconscious and that's it."

My mother, who was not present that weekend but was home in the East Bay Area, pulled a few pieces of the story from me. It took her a week to drag out enough pieces to get a skimpy picture. My father denied to her that anything out of the ordinary had happened, and he still denies it to this day. Although I felt that I could not tell anyone about the drowning and near-death experience, I held its memory in my heart as a treasure.

I learned that plans existed for me and that I had altered those plans by suicide. I could (or must?) go back. There was much to do. I remember not exactly wanting to leave, but not resisting either. Having seen the other side, I complied agreeably somehow and was imparted with these words. "Show them the way."

We spoke through our minds—not verbally. There were no buildings or streets there, just lots of sky and the most beautiful colors that can be imagined. As we walked, I saw miles and miles of people standing there. I couldn't make out anyone, there was like a cloud covering them. Then I heard God say, "You have to go back." I begged Him to please let me stay and again they repeated, "You have to go back." The next thing I knew, I woke up out of a coma.

Examples of Feeling State (Excerpts):

I feel completely drained of energy.

More and more intense feelings and cravings for soulful growth and refection.

Spontaneous tears of joy and some flashbacks or residual aftermath feelings also saturated my awareness in the first few weeks.

I am in the darkness alone, but not afraid.

Some kind of relief flooded over me when I heard a voice say, "You are dead! It's OK!"

I also felt the presence of a being. With this presence was a feeling of love the magnitude of which cannot be expressed. I have never known such peace, contentment and most important, love.

I am loved for who I am in the darkness, but I want to be more than loved. I want to love and be loved, to feel and be felt without justification.

There was no fear of anything because I knew the true answer to everything.

There seemed to be a lot of answers, but people's mouths did not move. Everyone was talking about home. All my troubles and worries went away and a peacefulness came over everything.

I felt no pain at all, I felt completely whole and free…I saw my physical body all crumpled and bloody and lifeless and this enormous wave of compassion washed over me.

I remember that a part of me felt frustrated and powerless to actually do anything of value—just as I have often felt in my physical body. Yet another part of me felt completely powerful, as though there was nothing that I couldn't accomplish…I remember feeling angry and fearful about going back.

My NDE happened as the result of a deliberate overdose in 1973. When I tried to kill myself, I was in deep despair and depression...I felt a tremendous feeling of rushing, speeding of myself towards a brilliant, warm, white, sparkly light...I felt surrounded by the most intense peace that I had ever experienced.

My heart rate accelerated. I began to sweat, and then to feel chilly, as my blood pressure fluctuated. I began to see flashes of various periods of my life...I could feel my heart throbbing in my chest.

I do not remember struggling or being afraid. I felt only deep peace and happiness. While my body was at the bottom of the river, I remember looking up towards the surface. I enjoyed watching a beautiful array of dancing, brilliant sparkles of color from the yellow sunlight coming through the river water. I was calm and fascinated by the beauty of the light and the reeds coming out of the mud. I also remember being wonderfully happy, peaceful, and excited at the same time. I stayed there in this bliss for a very long time.

I felt like I was floating in a void of lightness and it felt peaceful; then I became agitated and said, "No, No, No." I felt like I was outside my body looking down as I heard the doctors say, "We lost her." I could see them putting stimulators on me to jerk a heart beat out of me...the next thing I knew, I felt a vacuum pulling me down into darkness. I said, "I have too much work to do yet in this lifetime!"

I felt that everything was right—as it should be. There was a purpose to everything. I felt knowledge and glimpsed Godhead, I guess. There was absolute understanding, absolute love, absolute peace.

I remember being amazed that I was not frightened; I had always thought it would be frightening to die. I felt amazingly calm as I watched my mother; I felt such pain for her...now I realize dying can be peaceful and not terrifying.

The feeling of love and peace was everything I ever wanted. I was truly home.

Examples of Behavioral Manifestations of NDE (Excerpts):

The experience was so deep, intense, and powerful I crumpled to my knees and then fell on the floor with tears of joy in my eyes. My body/spirit could not handle any more of this overpowering immersion. It was like a 220 current frazzling a 110 socket. It almost became unbearable, the huge wave after wave of exquisite joy, communion, presence of the divine fused with a limited human being...

Some kind of relief flooded over me when I heard a voice say, "You are dead! It's OK!" Instantly I was transported to a new place, leaving my body behind on the ER table. I flew effortlessly through the ceiling and found myself standing in a magnificent field of tall grass. The grass was glistening, glowing in a slight breeze. The colors of the sky and grass were such that I had never seen before…I was dancing with my mother…we did not talk, only danced. We were incredibly happy.

I slowly climb higher and higher towards this light. I must reach this light before it is too late, too late for what? I don't know…I am at peace, floating towards a light that is more essential to me than anything else that I reach out for. I am alone…it is as if I am walking in a desert alone, even though there is sand beneath my feet and a bush here and there.

This darkness is all about me. There is no place to run. I am aware of all, but I do not have any physical movements, no energy to move, whether motor activity or animation. I am frozen in place.

Immediately after the impact from falling, I felt myself floating up, out of my body, and hovering above my body. All of the people who were watching seemed paralyzed by shock and horror. I remember looking down and seeing my body three-dimensionally for the first time.

Beginning in my early 20s the car crashes began, 17 to date. Of course, I wondered if I could have prevented the crashes. Was I distracted or sleepy or careless? Both the car insurance company and I never found them to be my fault. I never suspected that I was repeatedly having blackouts. So I took classes in defensive driving.

In 1982, I was 18 years old and had been seeking help with alcohol and speed abuse. My friend gave me some drugs one particular day. I felt good the first few hours of the day. That night, I began feeling numb and a feeling of dying slowly came over me. I remember hearing bells and (seeing) a slight vision of light coming towards me. I do remember hearing strange noises and I felt a certain spirit coming over me. I began to scream and fight for consciousness. I gripped my hands tightly together and gradually I came out of near-death.

In November, 1975, I drove into a wall. I remember as my jaw hit the steering wheel, I said, "Oh shit! I'm dead!" and then I was…I was surrounded by light so intense I could feel it. I could not look, it just sort of permeated me.

I had been having neurological problems and had been diagnosed as having myasthenia gravis (turned out I didn't). But at the time I was the most ill, I had lost use of many muscle groups and was rushed to emergency. I was feeling very weird and was having trouble talking. I don't really know what happened next except, all of a sudden, I was floating horizontally up by the ceiling. I looked down and could see my mother sitting by the side of the bed towards my feet…I could see what was happening, but it was veiled.
I became separate from my body and floated to the ceiling. I looked down at the body stretched across the table and I realized it was my body. I then became about four or five years old and floated straight up in an incredible light that surrounded me softly. It was like sunlight and a smoke-like mist filled with the smell of roses. There was Jesus standing there, bigger than life, with his right arm extended waiting for me. I bounced on giant-size dark red roses that smelled beautiful. I reached towards Jesus and He took me by my hand.

Examples of Overall Effects of the NDE (Excerpts):

My spiritual development and personal development over the past several years since my experience has been my top priority in life. Learning about our divine dialogue and personal relationship is a key commitment and focus. We are here on this earth to celebrate life, to love and help one another, and to tap into and use all the gifts and talents our creator has endowed us with.

It took me many years to fully process this event. Initially, I did not share my experience with anyone for fear they would think I was strange...over the years, I have been more and more impressed at my total lack of fear of death. This feeling also extends itself into a lack of interest in many of this life's realities. For instance, I have been totally unimpressed with people's feelings of self importance. I have realized that hierarchies are only man-made. They mean essentially nothing. I realize that someone or something (I call God or Goddess) has special understanding of each of us, has plans for each of us that we need to carry out to be fully realized.

If I have learned nothing else from my own experience and the ancient experiences of tradition, it is this: the purpose of the tradition is to teach each individual how to die without being killed or committing suicide. If any individual takes his own life or allows others to do it for him, then he will return and repeat the whole process again. If any individual seeks to live life fully and then dies *not through his own design*, then he will not return to repeat the whole process again.

This was a God of absolute, unconditional love I communicated with. It had no sex or form. Does love have a gender or physical form on this our human plane? I know now that our spirits will continue when we "die" from this earthly form.

I believe I overdosed and died, but for "His" reasons, God brought me back. From that day on, I know that physical death is not the ending, but the beginning of something so great that it transcends our understanding which is limited to our finite five senses. Being able to tell my story has been the most positive thing that has happened since my experience.

Most people who have an NDE return not only with their personal lives changed, but also return (with) a special purpose to carry out. The mission given to me is in three parts: one is to tell people who are dying or who have already passed over that there is truly nothing to fear. We only shed our bodies like a butterfly sheds its cocoon. There is no death. Secondly, fear is a man-made emotion. Thirdly, be very careful of religious leaders or teachers who say that this person or that person will not get into heaven because they are this or that. The law of God is written in each of our hearts...there are many pathways to God.

This experience impacted me mostly in a positive way, but there was some depression because I "wanted to be there." Sometimes I dream about my experience and I feel myself vibrating and then wake up.

This experience led me to be more open about my sexuality.

Although my NDE was a peak experience, the circumstances that caused the NDE (Guillian-Barre Syndrome) were most unpleasant. Since my NDE experience, my attitude, concept, and experience of spirituality increased, but I have no interest in pursuing spirituality. I am cautious and careful about sharing my NDE experience. I only share it with people who might appreciate it and only at the right time and circumstances.

I realized life was about risk and openness and honesty. I had been afraid for years of the labels lesbian and gay. I believe now that a nonsexual entity of all love exists for all time for all of us. We are watched over and guided and cared for always. We are never alone before or after death. I believe we are messengers to tell others the path is safe, loving, and (there is) nothing to fear.

I'm not sure I understand what happened to me, except that it launched me on a quest for meaning in the rest of my life.

I became much more open and unafraid to express my feelings and emotions.

Positive changes, I believe, including my intelligence, openness to new ideas and change, no fear at all, naïve and simple.

Until my late twenties, I was aware of a black hole in my center, never telling anyone about it until my fifties. Whenever I would become aware of it, I felt great fear. Now I believe that the black hole was near-death, which for me has been the most beautiful and peaceful experience in my life.

My near-death experience made me feel like I had a purpose here on earth, a destiny, that I had not yet fulfilled. It made me feel important.

In this experience, I have learned I have a purpose, something important I'm supposed to do for society. I learned that death feels wonderful. I know there is another dimension that I can access if I need to. I feel like there is something special about me. At times, I feel like an observer, even when I'm participating. Today, I am a teacher and it feels like I'm where I'm supposed to be. I fight injustices daily and teach kids to respect each other. I feel like I'm doing my part to "heal the world."

Next, I turned away and communication began with what others call a gatekeeper or angel or Jesus. It was someone. If I ever knew, I cannot remember now. I heard that God depends on us to work on earth. Intervention was not an option, somehow. I heard that actually there is no purgatory and no hell. People who leave too soon or hurt others may (must?) watch what effect their actions have on others. Time is so different there. Watching the results can be painful, I understood, but I did not understand it to be mandatory. I just understood it—no heaven or hell. The good ones get to watch, too.

I guess what I am learning with a great deal of difficulty is not to take on the pain of others—no matter who they are. I can feel compassion and try to help, but will not be led by my emotions and feelings which gets me into major trouble. The other thing I am now learning on a daily basis is to love myself and hold myself with tenderness and know that I am truly a child of God and that I am loved and deserve to have a life of quality. I am also learning with a great deal of difficulty not to give my power away to anyone else and (to) listen to my own intuition.

During my experience, I learned that God loves me just the way I am. I am learning to love myself. It took me many years to really realize what did happen to me and I am so grateful to be back to speak out to people. After my experience, I shared it with only two or three people and they said I was crazy. I stopped talking about it and didn't go out for many years after this. I always had trouble integrating in this world. In 1990, when I was dying on my kitchen floor, God came to me and told me to get up and speak out. I have been running around speaking about God and Jesus and functioning to the best of my ability. I have been enjoying life, family, and friends, seeing things and going to places I haven't seen before. I love church and worshipping God and praying all the time.

BIBLIOGRAPHY

Atwater, P.M.H. *Beyond The Light*. NY: Birch Lane Press, 1994. Compilation of NDE research, synthesizing the entire field.

Atwater, P.M.H. *Future Memory*. NY: Birch Lane Press, 1996. The ability to "pre-live" the future.

Chopra, Deepak. *Everyday Immortality*. NY: Harmony Books, 1999. Spiritual transformation.

De la Huerta, Christian. *Coming Out Spiritually*. NY: Jeremy D. Tarcher/Putnam, 1999. A guide to reclaim a spiritual connection for gays and lesbians.

Eadie, Betty. *Embraced By The Light*. Placerville, CA: Gold Leaf Press, 1992.

Easwaran, Eknath. *Dialogue With Death*. Petaluma, CA: Nilgiri Press, 1981. An intriguing look into the experience of death and its meaning.

Foster, Jean. *Epilogue*. MO: UNISUN, 1988. A channeled book about the next plane of life.

Grof, Stanislav and Grof, Christina (ed). *Spiritual Emergency*. NY: Putnam Books, 1989. About personal transformation through spiritual emergencies and beyond.

Grof, Stanislav and Grof, Christina. *Beyond Death*. London: Thames and Hudson, 1980. Concepts of the afterlife including survivors of clinical death accounts.

Grof, Stanislav. *The Adventure Of Self-Discovery*. Albany, NY: State University of New York Press, 1988. The dimensions of inner explorations.

Kircher, Pamela. *Love Is The Link*. Burdett, NY: Larson Publications, 1995. A hospice physician writes about the NDE, death, and dying.

Kubler-Ross, Elizabeth. *The Tunnel and The Light*. NY: Marlowe & Company, 1999. Essential insights on living and dying.

Moody, Raymond and Perry, Paul. *Reunions*. NY: Ivy Books, 1993. About visionary encounters with departed loved ones.

Moody, Raymond. *Life After Life*. Covington, GA: Mockingbird Books, 1975. Now being distributed by Bantam Books.

Moody, Raymond. *The Last Laugh*. Charlottesville, VA: Hampton Roads Publishing Company, 1999. "Empathic near-death experience" is explored.

Morse, Melvin and Perry, Paul. *Closer To The Light*. NY: Ivy Books, 1990. Interviews with children about the end of life and "something" that survives bodily death.

Mother Meera. *Mother Meera Answers*. Ithaca, NY: Meeramma Publications, 1991. The transformative power of divine light.

Mullin, Glenn. *Death And Dying*. London and NY: Arkana, 1987. A book about nine Tibetan texts examining death and dying.

Ring, Ken and Valarino, Evelyn. *Lessons From The Light*. NY and London: Insight Books, 1998. Shows those who have not had an NDE what it is.

Steiger, Brad and Steiger, Sherry. *Children Of The Light*. NY: Signet, 1995. Children who passed over to the other side.

Sunderman, Marilyn. *Past Lives, Present Joy*. NY: Kensington Books, 1999. A soul's journey from one lifetime to the next.

Sutherland, Cherie. *Within The Light*. NY: Bantam Books, 1995. NDE experience.

Thich Nhat Hanh. *The Miracle Of Mindfulness*. Boston: Beacon Press, 1975. A beautiful book on meditation, concentration, relaxation.

Thich Nhat Hanh. *Touching Peace*. Berkeley, CA: Parallax Press, 1992. The art of mindful living.

Thich Nhat Hanh. *Going Home*. NY: Riverhead Books, 1999. Central teachings of Buddhism and Christianity.

Van Praagh, James. *Talking To Heaven*. NY: Dutton 1997. About life after death.

Weiss, Brian. *Many Lives, Many Masters*. NY: Fireside Book, 1988. Past life therapy.

Weiss, Brian. *Only Love Is Real*. NY: Warner Books, 1996. A story of soulmates reunited.

Wilbur, Ken. *Grace and Grit*. Boston and London: Shambhala, 1991. An experience of sacred partnership.

When Ego Dies: A Compilation Of Near-Death and Mystical Conversion Experiences. Houston, TX: Emerald Ink Publishing, 1996. Houston IANDS members tell their stories "in their own words."

OTHER TITLES BY EMERALD INK

Business & Home

Debt Control, Chris Richards, ISBN 1-885373-19-8
Start A Business Without Borrowing, D. Kelly Irvin, ISBN 1-885373-05-8
The Network Marketer, Forrest Watson, PhD, ISBN 1-885373-37-6
Understanding & Reducing Your Home Electric Bill, Richard L. Hepburn, MS, ISBN 1-885373-01-5

Crime

Houston Knights Undercover, J. D. Dan Cargill, ISBN 1-885373-39-2

Health

Brain Damage, Dick Schmelzkopf, ISBN 1-885373-34-1
Conquering Kids' Cancer, Ken Lazaraus, MD, ISBN 1-885373-22-8
How I Conquered Cancer (naturopathic prostate), Eric Gardiner, ISBN 1-885373-11-2
How I Conquered Cancer, Eric Gardiner Audio ISBN 1-555373-16-3
Manic Depression: How To Live While Loving a Manic Depressive, Lynn Bradley, ISBN 1-885373-28-7
Sexual Health, Doris Zale, RN, ISBN 1-885373-26-0

History/Memoirs/Travel/Ghosts

China Mailbag Uncensored, Lou Glist, ISBN 1-885373-21-X
Reflections of A Rotarian, Jack Pearce, ISBN 1-885373-03-1
Sorceress of the Trade Winds (poor French immigrant to US rises to top), Claude Isnard, ISBN 1-885373-08-2
Spirits of Texas (true Texas ghosts), Vallie Fletcher Taylor, ISBN 1-885373-40-6
They Sent Me An Invitation So I Went To WW II (CBI-India), Bill James, ISBN 1-885373-15-5

Social

It's U-Mail! A Lighthearted Guide to Enhancing Your Intuition, Linda Fike and Robert Stecker, PhD, ISBN 1-885373-20-1
Love Now—Here's How (removing roadblocks to relationships), Phyllis Light, PhD, ISBN 1-885373-36-8
Prince Charming Lives, Phyllis Light, PhD, ISBN 1-885373-38-4
Society & Sex Offenders, Ray Mullen, MSW, ISBN 1-885373-14-7

Spiritual

Crossing Over & Coming Home (gay/lesbian NDEs), Liz Dale, PhD, ISBN 1-885373-32-5
Holy Man, Holy War (fictional narrative of revolutionary Jesus), Fred Berry, ISBN 1-885373-10-4
Mary of Galilee (narrative of early life of Mary), Woodard, ISBN 1-885373-23-6
Memory of Elsewhere (reflections on meaning), Rona Murray, PhD, ISBN 1-885373-35-X
To Hell And Back (fundamentalist NDE), Don Brubaker, Audio 1-885373-17-1
You Know Me—The Gita (Bhagavad Gita), tr. Irina Gajjar, PhD, ISBN 1-885373-27-9
When Ego Dies-A Compilation of Near-Death & Mystical Conversion Stories, ISBN 1-885373-07-4

Emerald Ink Publishing
9700 Almeda Genoa #502
Houston, Texas 77075
(800) 324-5663
emerald@emeraldink.com
http://www.emeraldink.com